TRIMURTI

THE PSYCHOLOGY OF LIFE

PRANAVA

Made with ♥ on the Notion Press Platform
www.notionpress.com

To Mumma, Papa, and my little sister, Gudda.
In our material existence, we walk on four different paths,
all leading to the same spiritual destination: the oneness
of family love.

"When it's an end, it's the end of a perception, which can again begin with the rise of a new perspective."

Har Har Mahadev.
To the pure soul in each individual.

Contents

Preface . . . . *xv*

Introduction . . . . *xxi*

1. THE CREATION OF TRIMURTI 1

1.1 Creation of Lord Brahma 2

1.2 Creation of Lord Vishnu 7

1.3 Creation of Lord Shiva the Liberator 11

1.4 Conclusion 16

2. THE BETTER HALF OF TRIMURTIS 21

2.1 Maa Saraswati 24

2.2 Maa Laxmi 27

2.3 Maa Sakthi 32

2.4 Conclusion 35

3. TRIMURTI IS THE SYMBOL OF BODY, MIND, AND SOUL 39

3.1 Lord Brahma is the Symbol of the Body 40

3.2 Lord Vishnu, the Symbol of the Mind 47

3.3 Lord Shiva is the Symbol of the Soul 52

3.4 Conclusion 56

4. IMPORTANCE OF TRIMURTI 59

4.1 Physical Fitness 60

4.2 Mental Awareness 63

4.3 Spiritual Awakening...............................67

4.4 Conclusion 70

5. YOGA TO EMBRACE TRIMURTI IN LIFE.................73

5.1 What is the Definition of Yoga? And Its Importance?.......74

5.2 Kriya Yoga 76

5.3 Jnana Yoga..78

5.4 Karma Yoga.......................................80

5.5 Bhakti Yoga 82

5.6 4-Step Daily Life Yoga 84

6. HELP FROM TRIMURTI 89

6.1 Visit Lord Brahma 90

6.2 Be Friends with Lord Vishnu.......................92

6.3 Find Lord Shiva 93

6.4 Conclusion 95

7. SPIRITUAL LOVE..................................97

7.1 Detachment 97

7.2 Sacrifice 99

7.3 Forgiveness 100

7.4 Selfless Love...101

7.5 Kindness 102

7.6 Spiritual Love 103

Acknowledgements *105*

Disclaimer

This book presents my personal interpretations and theories regarding the Trimurti gods—Brahma, Vishnu, and Shiva—as symbols of the body, mind, and soul. The perspectives and insights shared herein are drawn from my own experiences and understanding and are not intended to represent the official teachings or doctrines of Hinduism or any other religious tradition.

Quotes from some famous people and from the Bhagavad Gita have been used to support and illustrate these interpretations. These quotations are intended to provide context and depth to my philosophical and psychological explorations. While I have taken great care to reference the Bhagavad Gita accurately, readers should consult the original texts and seek guidance from knowledgeable sources for a more comprehensive understanding.

This book is meant to inspire reflection and personal growth. It is not intended as a substitute for professional medical, psychological, or spiritual advice. Readers are encouraged to approach the content with an open mind and consider their own beliefs and experiences in relation to the ideas presented.

The interpretations and opinions expressed in this book are solely those of the author and do not necessarily reflect the views of any religious or spiritual organisation. Additionally, I wish to emphasise that this work is intended to respect and honour the beliefs surrounding the Bhagavad Gita and Hinduism. It is not my intention to offend or diminish the significance of these sacred traditions in any way.

Preface

In early childhood, I was diagnosed with a learning disability, which was just the beginning of a chaotic journey of my life, which started through academics and personal struggles. As a result, in my late teenage years, I found solace in drugs and alcohol. Dealing with traumas immaturely and seeking stability in the confused life of intoxication. The greatest agony of my life was not being able to express the real feelings of the lost soul inside me who wanted to dance, which can express the whole universe in it, play like a pro, be a confident extrovert, and be awesome in whatever I could. But I was always trapped in the chaos of depressed shadows of not being able to express my inner world correctly to my outer world. My life was stuck between the confusion of my inner paradise and outer reality.

Because of heavy intoxication and some other mental traumas, such as not being able to perform well in academics and other immature life dealings, at the age of 22, I was diagnosed with schizophrenia and other multiple mental illnesses like hypomania, paranoia, psychasthenia, and hypochondriasis. These are highly chaotic mental disorders an ordinary mind can have, most related to psychotic fears. Because of this, I was on shock treatment and had been given 25-30 shocks overall. After the discharge, the chaotic journey multiplied into something very terrible, and I ended up suffering from these mental illnesses along with psychotic depression and social anxiety for ten years of my life and many times getting admitted to mental hospitals and was on psychotic medications. At the same time, coping immaturely with alcohol and drug abuse. But fighting with my challenges made me learn something new from each fatal fall that happened.

Which made me always feel that something was lost so that something could be found. But then what is lost and what is found, which I had or which I have? Nothing. Things come and go; you stop, you walk, you run, and you do whatever you want in life. It will always be fruitful when you try to learn something positive at every moment of your great life. A time-freeze also teaches you the biggest lesson of life: patience. So, nothing is wasted in this life.

In this ten-year-long chaotic frozen journey, one thing that helped me was lots of "whys," which appeared because of observation and searching for ways to solve the "whys" that appeared in my mind. I have always wished that it would be amazing if I could manage to be a psychologist since childhood when I used to visit a psychologist because of my learning disability problems. I found their job very cool because these people knew how the mind works and why people behave the way they act. Still, I never considered pursuing it because of my lower academic performance. So, I took my mental illness as an opportunity to learn about the psychology of the mind and started observing minor things about the mind. This created more panic and chaos in my mind because I used to feel what was happening. Still, I knew what was happening was not sane and unrelated to reality. It was illusions and delusions of unreal chaotic fears that felt real. I just kept fighting to take control of my mind every day for these ten years. I never succeeded until last year when I got this gift, Trimurti, the psychological theory of life through the quotes of Shrimad Bhagavad Gita in a philosophical way from Lord Ganesha on 28 September 2023 on Ganapati visirjan.

A confused person is not confused because of confusion. The confusion is confusing him in understanding the reason behind the confusion; if a confused person knows that he is confused, then is he really confused? If not, then what is confusing him? Isn't it confusing? Yes, indeed. The only thing that stands between confusion and clarity is your inner control over your outer reality.

In 2017, when I was also dealing with paranoid schizophrenia and psychotic depression, I encountered the suicide of my newly met friend who seemed very strong physically and mentally but hanged himself and died by suicide. After that, four to five friends of mine who appeared more physically and mentally fit than me died by suicide. This showed me that you cannot judge someone's inner world based on their outer appearance. Eventually, I heard about the Blue Whale game. The first thing that came to my mind was if someone could program a game of mind destruction to the extent that it could influence young children to kill themselves. It ensured I would do something to help mentally disturbed people build excellent and healthy minds.

The essential aspect of this journey was the Bhagavad Gita quotes. From the start, I always had the Bhagavad Gita app on my mobile if I had one because, on this long journey, I lost multiple mobile phones, and most of the time, I didn't have a phone with me. But when I had a mobile, there used to be the Bhagavad Gita app. In my very darkest mental breakdown, I used to open that app, and some quotes used to pop up randomly as a quote of the day. They used to solve my problem at that particular moment. When I tried to understand the Bhagavad Gita, I always wondered why Hinduism, the first religion in the world, only had three main deities to worship. I then started searching for my answers.

What is in the whys that make you an interesting person? The different ways you walk on to find your unique whys make you an interesting person.

Through introspection and deep research into psychology and spirituality, I found a guiding light in the Trimurti gods of Hinduism. It was as if every piece of wisdom collected by my lost soul over the years had just come together, giving me the ultimate psychology of human life, which shaped me to be the best version of myself.

Knowing and following this theory about body, mind, and soul helped me overcome my severe mental problems like paranoid schizophrenia and psychotic depression. Along with this journey, I managed to become a government and United Nations-certified psychotherapist and hypnotherapist.

The primary purpose behind writing this book is to give a psychological understanding of the energy auras of Trimurti gods, the Sanatana Dharma, in a philosophical way that can solve your life problems, which have solved my extremely chaotic mental disorders.

I am not suggesting anything about miracles that can happen when you follow whatever I suggest in this book about physical, mental, and spiritual well-being, which is connected to Hinduism's three main deities, the Sanatana Dharma: Lord Brahma, Lord Vishnu, and Lord Shiva. Still, I can guarantee that without any miracle, you will live a happy, joyful, and liberated life just by understanding this theory and using it in your daily lives.

It's not the magic that surprises you. It's the assumption of the trick that hits you with how it happened surprises you; life's ultimate fun is not watching the magic but performing it by yourself.

Whatever wisdom is written in this book is not taken from any guru's guidance. It is abstracted from the Bhagavad Gita and various ideas and stories of the Hindu gods and goddesses. This helped me overcome such a chaotic mind, and I am sure that it will solve your life problems, too.

The best way to understand God is to have freedom of faith, which my religion, Hinduism, the Sanatana Dharma, gives me. One can have different faiths about God. Applying this privilege given by my religion to have an independent understanding of God and goddesses, that they reside in every particle of the universe. Exploring so many different ideas of worshipping them and being culturally blessed with beautiful stories of various gods and goddesses, which I have been listening to throughout my childhood. It eventually helped me gain some unique wisdom about the three principal deities of Sanatana Dharma. I am connecting to the Bhagavad Gita and all the stories and wisdom about Hindu gods and goddesses and putting them into the correct chronology. I have reached a philosophical journey that can help you understand the psychology of life, which is hidden in the existence of the psychology of Trimurti.

Introduction

Life's ultimate truth of energy is hidden in this Sanskrit line from Rig Veda.

"Ekam sat vipra bahuda vadanti," meaning "Truth is one; the wise call it by different names," highlights that there is a single, universal truth underlying all existence. Despite diverse expressions and interpretations across cultures and religions, this phrase emphasises that all perspectives point to the same ultimate reality. It encourages respect for different beliefs and fosters an inclusive understanding of spiritual and philosophical truths.

In this book, you will understand why only Hinduism, the Sanatana Dharma, has three main deities and their valuable role in daily life. You will also learn how these three came into existence, creating themselves through a single energy source.

Every individual carries masculine and feminine energies in themselves, regardless of gender. Understanding the profound psychological explanation of why Lord Brahma's wife is Maa Saraswati, why Lord Vishnu's wife is Maa Laxmi, and why Lord Shiva's wife is Maa Sakthi (Parvati), and how all these dimensions of gods and goddesses exist in a single you and how balancing them internally can make your external life run smoothly and happily.

In the book, you will explore the balance between masculine and feminine energy forces in physical, mental, and spiritual well-being in every individual, regardless of gender, through the philosophical wisdom of the Trimurti gods, which will explain the psychological trilogy of life.

I have used three terms: Lord Brahma, which refers to the creation aspects and body. Lord Vishnu refers to the people who were the preservers, propagators, and minds. Lord Shiva refers to people who lived detached lives and helped other people liberate themselves from their emotional problems while connecting to the inner self and soul.

The journey in the book clearly explains why Sanatana Dharma is called the way of life. Why are the three main deities not just to worship but something bigger than that. Trimurti means three symbols, and each symbol has a meaning behind it. The symbol of Lord Brahma represents body and physical fitness, the symbol of Lord Vishnu represents mind and mental awareness, and the symbol of Lord Shiva represents soul and spiritual awakening.

Rather than just praying to God, these symbols represent the balanced ways life one needs to embrace for a happy and successful life. Every essence of life given in this book is about one individual, regardless of gender. Every dimension of Trimurti and their wives is present in you, and by balancing them, you can lead a happy, sane, and serene life.

This book's starting point is energy intelligence, and before starting, I would like to share some of the quotes given by very famous people about energy that relate to the book's content.

Albert Einstein: "Energy cannot be created or destroyed; it can only be changed from one form to another."

Thomas Edison: "We are like tenant farmers chopping down the fence around our house for fuel when we should be using Nature's inexhaustible sources of energy—sun, wind, and tide."

Nikola Tesla: "My brain is only a receiver; in the Universe, there is a core from which we obtain knowledge, strength, and inspiration."

Nikola Tesla: "If you want to find the secrets of the universe, think in terms of energy, frequency, and vibration."

Energy is what we feel, and what we feel is life. If what we feel in life is the definition of life, then it can also be the definition of energy.

Let's explore the discovered spiritual side of life's energy psychology in philosophical ways, which will ultimately give pure essence to the great human life.

HAR HAR MAHADEV...

CHAPTER 1

The Creation of Trimurti

Understanding the trilogy of Trimurti - Lord Brahma, the creator. Lord Vishnu, the preserver. Lord Shiva, the destroyer, will reveal their roles beyond their titles. Lord Brahma not only creates but also stabilises his creation, ensuring the balance and harmony of life. Lord Vishnu preserves and propagates life, nurturing and sustaining the world. And Lord Shiva destroys and liberates, paving the way for a higher taste in life. These roles of the Trimurti are deeply intertwined with the creation, preservation, and liberation of life, connecting us to the spiritual essence of Hinduism, the Sanatana Dharma.

It is going to begin with energy intelligence. Everything in this universe is made up of energy. You and I are also made up of energy, which is tangible energy that has earthly elements. There is also energy around us that we cannot see through the human eye. If everything in the universe has a specific intelligence to reform and transform, then why doesn't energy have intelligence? We can observe energy intelligence in mystical forces and vibrations present in the environment that sometimes help you mystically and mysteriously when you are having a problem while exposing yourself to certain things that give you the idea of how to solve it or unknowingly encountering people who help you in a particular situation. This energy is beyond scepticism. Many people may have experienced this energy at some point in their lives. According to that, people have given different names to that energy, like gods, demigods, angels, luck, manifestation, the law of attraction, destiny, and many more. Same work, many names, and through that energy, everything is created. That energy I refer to as Lord Brahma, who is the creator and beyond scepticism as described in the Vedas.

1.1 Creation of Lord Brahma

Before life as we know it, when only energies existed, some of these energies came together and developed intelligence. This is akin to a plant growing in a suitable environment without any specific planting. The same principle applies to these primordial energies. Through their inherent intelligence of creation, these energies formed the first single-cell life on Earth when the environment was conducive. This life form gradually evolved into more complex forms. The energy that was formed into material existence was Lord Brahma, the creator of life in Hindu cosmology.

This concept aligns with themes found in ancient Hindu texts like the Rigveda and the Upanishads, and modern scientific theories such as the Big Bang and abiogenesis.

Bhagavad Gita, chapter 14, verse 3: The Great Nature is My womb; in that, I (the ultimate one) place the seed of life, and thence are born all beings.

In this quote, the womb and seed refer to the same individual energy. This quote conveys what I want to say in the above passage.

Renowned works on ancient wisdom, consciousness, and quantum connection reveal that material energy is guided and shaped by spiritual energy and its vibrations, which can be defined as Lord Brahma, the ultimate truth. This energy is divided into two forms: spiritual and material. Spiritual energy is present in the environment, and material energy is life on Earth made by earthly elements. Material energy represents physical life and has the power to contribute to the development of life consciously. Spiritual energy, on the other hand, guides material energy throughout its existence. Spiritual energy is pure and neutral because it doesn't carry the earthly material senses to experience negativity or positivity. When material energy dies and exists, it transforms into spiritual energy. This spiritual energy then utilises the knowledge gained from its previous material life to guide new material energies through putting circumstances in their life to evolve and develop, participating in the grand evolution of life. This simplifies the idea that when you and I die, we will be part of a spiritual energy that contains knowledge and wisdom gained from material life.

Bhagavad Gita, chapter 15, verse 16: As the Vedas say, "There are two classes of beings, the fallible and the infallible. In the material world, everyone is fallible, and in the spiritual world, everyone is infallible."

This quote defines and differentiates the material and spiritual energy I am discussing.

We can compare this concept to the example of a plant. The suitable, fertile environment that allows the plant to grow represents spiritual energy. Plants grow and contribute to the world by producing oxygen and many things that embody material energy. When the plant dies, it becomes a source of fertility, transforming back into spiritual energy that supports the growth of new plants. This cycle illustrates how material energy contributes to the world and returns to spiritual power, aiding in the ongoing evolution of life.

Many near-death experiences, Quantum Consciousness, energy transformation, consciousness transference theories, and books define that material energy is transferred to spiritual energy after death.

Brahma's spiritual and material energies took millions of years to evolve into humans—an advanced, social, and intelligent species with exceptional cognitive abilities.

This aligns with scientific understanding, acknowledging that species took millions of years to evolve into modern humans. So, after years of evolution through the coordination of spiritual and material energy, humans were developed as intelligent and social animals.

Lord Brahma is said to be omnipresent and omniscient worldwide because it formed life after millions of years of calculation, and it knows its every essence.

We are Lord Brahma's material energy, capable of feeling and consciously contributing to the ever-evolving life. The spiritual energy of Lord Brahma, which has the correct wisdom to guide you without any attachments, is a mystical force of vibrations that shapes us and helps us in mysterious ways.

The great essence of referring to Lord Brahma is the energy intelligence given in the Bhagavad Gita Chapter 13, verses 14-15-16-17-18, which describes Lord Brahma's hands, legs, eyes, face, and ears are everywhere. He is all-pervading, the original source of all the senses, but he has no senses. Though detached, he maintains all existence. Though he controls all three modes of material nature, he is beyond modes. He exists inside and outside of everything, moving and non-moving. He is beyond material comprehension or recognition. He is far and also near. He is indivisible, though he appears divided among all living beings. He is the supreme creator, maintainer, and annihilator. He is the source of light and luminaries, beyond the darkness of ignorance. He is knowledge, the object of knowledge, and also the goal of knowledge. He lives in everyone's heart.

And this wisdom clearly describes Lord Brahma as the energy intelligence according to the Bhagavad Gita.

No one has any specific tangible evidence of this unknown intelligent energy force, but many of us believe in such power and have given it different names. It's unbelievable that the solar system is like a carefully balanced dance. The planets revolve around the Sun just the right way, held in place by gravity. Earth's tilt and distance from the Sun create the seasons and make life possible. Even the Moon helps by stabilising Earth's movements. If anything changes even a little, it could throw everything out of balance into chaotic destruction. This shows how small changes can have significant impacts. This also gives essence to understanding that energy has intelligence, which means Lord Brahma.

So, the very essence of this wisdom is collected from various studies and understanding from Bhagavad Gita's perspective. That the Lord Brahma is everywhere, inside and outside, part of everything, and is also the supreme controller. So, let's explore what happened when intelligent humans were created.

1.2 Creation of Lord Vishnu

According to Hinduism, Lord Vishnu's avatars play a crucial role in preserving life on Earth and propagating new ideas for a happy, sane, and smooth existence. Human records indicate that human existence spans 200,000 to 300,000 years, with civilisation records emerging only a few thousand years ago. This raises the question: were there no preservers and propagators before this period? The existence and development of our older ancestors from 4,000 to 5,000 years ago, of which we have records, would not have been possible without the preservation and propagation of life by those who lived thousands of years before them.

Let's explore this step by step. When intelligent humans with advanced cognitive abilities first emerged, their primary concerns were survival, shelter, food, and safety. They began to revere natural elements such as rivers, seas, skies, and trees as gods, believing these forces had mystical powers to guide them in mysterious ways. This reverence can be seen as an early worship of Lord Brahma or God.

To protect themselves from predatory animals, humans formed groups for mutual survival. Each group had leaders, or alphas, who made critical decisions to preserve and propagate the group's well-being. The alphas typically had strong mental and physical abilities suited to the group's needs.

Different groups began merging and forming larger communities as time passed, making life more manageable and accessible. However, this combination meant only one leader could emerge for the entire group. This situation led to challenges where strong alpha-like personalities had to undergo mental and physical tests designed by the elders and previous leaders of the group. Their prior leaders and parents used to train alpha-like personalities to ensure they could become kings and effectively guide the unified group.

The king's primary role is to preserve and propagate his society, maintaining political and friendly alliances with other groups. However, if a king exhibits demonic behaviour and disrupts the people's peaceful and happy lives, society needs someone to address this threat. In such cases, Lord Vishnu plays a crucial role by intervening to restore balance and order.

A parallel process occurs when parents with higher privileges train their children. Some individuals, often from unprivileged backgrounds or maybe from privileged backgrounds, were the same as kings but had wise minds and a love for humanity. They were trained by the mystical, spiritual energy of Lord Brahma by throwing life's difficulties on them. These individuals, who built their strength and wisdom from challenging experiences, were deeply connected to humanity and self-trained. They emerge as the ones who challenge and overcome the demonic-like personality kings. These individuals are often seen as embodiments of Lord Vishnu, who restores balance and harmony. And it's not specifically about men. If the woman does that work, she will be considered Lord Vishnu.

So, basically, whoever in the world took the responsibility to preserve and propagate life regardless of gender in any place could be considered Lord Vishnu, as understood in the Bhagavad Gita.

Bhagavad Geeta, chapter 4, verses 7-8: Whenever there is a gross decline in righteousness and an increase in unrighteousness, O Arjun, I manifest myself on Earth at that time. To protect the righteous, annihilate the wicked, and re-establish Dharma's principles, I appear on this Earth, age after age.

The primary energy of the great Lord Vishnu takes birth when there are great difficulties, like Lord Vishnu's great avatars. Still, it is also Lord Vishnu's Dharma to preserve and propagate minor disruptions in the world. We can understand this through the sayings of Swami Vivekananda's understanding from the above quote of Bhagavad Gita, where he explains that whenever evil and immorality prevail, I body myself forth. For the protection of the good, the destruction of the wicked, and the establishment of Dharma, I come into being in every age.

Whenever the world goes down, the Lord comes to help it forward, and so He does from time to time and place to place. In explaining this, he added that whenever evil and immorality prevail on Earth, He will come down and support His children, which He is doing from time to time and from place to place. And whenever you see an extraordinary holy man trying to uplift humanity, know He is in him. This saying gives the essence to this whole understanding.

It's wise to understand that there is a preserver and propagator in each step of life and its existence. Starting from our house. There is a person who holds the authority in decision-making because everybody respects them and their wisdom. This smoothly preserves and propagates the family. Then, there is someone in the building, the area, the district, the city, the state, and the country. Maybe one's authority and the work of these individuals may vary. However, the responsibilities are the same; no duty is big or small. Duty is duty if all of them are doing the same duty. Why cannot we count them equally? According to whoever perseveres and propagates nice things in life in whichever aspect they are, we should call them a symbolic presentation of Lord Vishnu, the preserver and propagator.

But preservation and propagation are not enough for society's people. We also need the help of Lord Shiva, who is known as the destroyer and liberator. Let's understand that.

1.3 Creation of Lord Shiva the Liberator

Lord Shiva is known as the destroyer in Hinduism. But I see Lord Shiva as the liberator from the wisdom I have accumulated in my journey. Let's see why.

Lord Vishnu was considered the God of their civilisation because of the immense intelligent work they contributed to running the civilisation wisely and smoothly and saving it from demonic intentions and destruction. When things started running smoothly, new evils entered human lives that were not tangible, and because of that, Lord Vishnu could not beat them in battlegrounds.

Along with civilisations' smooth, manageable lives, humans were divided into four elementary classes, which were required to run a civilisation according to the abilities and intelligence one carried to do the job. The first class consisted of society's kings, leaders, and gurus. The second class consisted of the army and police. The third class consisted of businessmen and other office staff. The fourth class consisted of labourers and workers.

But because of that, a new problem occurred in humans' lives. New mighty evils came into existence. They were very powerful and were the ones Lord Vishnu couldn't fight directly to defeat because they were not tangible yet very destructive in reality. These were the negative emotions and feelings like guilt, grief, shame, anger, sadness, anxiety, etc. Every class of human tends to suffer from at least one emotional problem. Kings, queens, or gurus commonly suffered from anger and sadness because they needed to direct people and impose limitations. The army and police may have suffered from grief, guilt, and sadness because they might have lost some of their fellow members in battles, affecting their families as well. Businessmen commonly face anxiety because business is inherently uncertain, and financial instability can be stressful. Lastly, workers may have felt shame and guilt because they were not as successful in providing a privileged life for their families, often due to their limited earnings.

Because individuals were facing emotional distress and dissatisfaction in their minds, the civilisations started becoming unmanageable and corrupt. People from the lower and middle classes showed rebellious attitudes, resorting to theft. Business people became fraudulent to earn extra income. Office workers got into gambling. Police and army personnel got addicted to intoxicants to overcome grief. Other leaders and gurus started playing political and mind games with each other. All this happened not because of some external force attacking civilisation but because people's internal emotions and feelings became the evils of their society.

However, a few strong people denied being corrupt because they thought corruption would lead to hurting other humans emotionally and physically, which they thought was an impure way of life. They detached themselves from civilisation and started living simple lives outside of it. Although detached from material luxuries and happiness, they found ways to be happy in a simple life. In that process, the mystical energies of Lord Brahma helped them discover yoga and meditation. They started connecting life with nature and its stillness, through which they connected to their innermost pure soul beyond material aspects. They found true happiness and never-ending ecstasy and bliss by linking to this fundamental part of Brahma's spiritual energy. Thus, they refused to hurt anyone for material pleasure and lived a detached and pure life while connecting to the pure soul within them. They called it "Shiva," and this word carries the same meaning in the world's oldest languages. In Sanskrit and Tamil, it signifies "auspicious" and "purity." In Sumerian, it means "god" or "spirit," and in ancient Egyptian, it is associated with "spirit" or "soul." Therefore, those who discovered and understood its profound essence came to be known as Lord Shiva.

The essence of this is given in Bhagavad Gita:
Chapter 5, verse 24: A yogi is happy within himself. He sees God within himself. He is flooded with self-enlightenment.

He attains liberation from material existence and unites with God.

Chapter 6, verses 20-23—In the stage of ultimate perfection called trance, or samādhi, one's mind is totally restrained from the material, mental activities by practising yoga. This perfection of action is characterised by one's ability to see the inner Self with the pure mind and to rejoice and relish in the Self.

Corruption led to a state of chaos in civilisation. We know Lord Vishnu was not attached to material aspects of life because whatever he did was for humanity and its evolution. Still, he could not detach himself from his authority because of his love for civilisation, and he could not leave his duty.

Just as some of us take a holiday when we feel stuck in life, Lord Vishnu may have distanced themselves from civilisation to find a way to defeat these evils. During this period, they discovered individuals who chose to live detached lives away from civilisation after encountering corruption arising from emotional problems. They were living a straightforward life, connecting to the pure soul within them through meditation, yoga, and other practices.

These individuals were also physically strong because they needed to protect themselves from wild animals. Therefore, they chose to live in the mountains where animals had difficulty reaching them. (This is another significance of why Lord Shiva and his followers used to meditate on mountains.) Lord Vishnu acknowledged that these were the ones who left civilisation because they did not want to be impure by hurting others or themselves due to their emotional problems.

When Lord Vishnu lived with these individuals and understood their way of life, they sought help from them to guide people facing emotional problems and evoke the essence of Lord Shiva in them. Alongside this, Lord Vishnu began to embrace Lord Shiva's path after they retired by transferring their roles as preservers and propagators to another Lord Vishnu. This transition inspired ordinary people to consider adopting the pure life of Lord Shiva.

We can metaphorically connect this with the Samudra Manthan story. Imagine Samudra Manthan as the civilisation created by Lord Vishnu. In this metaphor, Lord Vishnu built a civilisation where everyone took the good things for themselves. However, during this process, the poison from Samudra Manthan represents the negative emotions and feelings that surfaced—corrupting the civilisation and leading it toward destruction. The simple and innocent individuals (Bhole) who sacrificed material happiness and desires by sacrificing and detaching themselves from regular life to live and lead a pure life. Akin to Lord Shiva's path are those who drank the poison, symbolising Lord Shiva's act of consuming the poison to protect the world.

1.4 Conclusion

This is how the three main auras of life were created. While no specific record identifies the first humans, it is scientific to understand that humans came into existence through evolution. Although there is no concrete evidence of spiritual energy guiding us, its existence is suggested by the commonality in how civilisations developed independently. Each has similar ideas and structures despite being on different continents.

The archetypal themes and symbols are shared across humanity. The wisdom that mystical energy might influence and guide the evolution of civilisations reflects a similar notion, where a shared, unseen force or intelligence contributes to the commonalities observed in human development and spiritual insights. There are many significant signs of this in many famous books and ideas about how energy and vibrational frequency shape human lives, which gives a clear idea about energy intelligence.

There is no specific evidence identifying who the first Lord Vishnu was in the world. However, interestingly, the avatars of Lord Vishnu mentioned in the Vedas align with Darwin's theory of evolution. This suggests we cannot pinpoint the exact time of Lord Vishnu's emergence. The concept of Vishnu appears to manifest in the evolving needs of different eras to preserve and propagate life. The presence of such transformative figures across various cultures and civilisations at similar times indicates that these archetypal entities emerge in response to the universal requirements of their respective ages.

Records of ancient cave art dating back 10,000 years show that early humans were deeply concerned with preserving and propagating life for their immediate survival and future generations. They developed sophisticated systems of knowledge, technology, and ethics to support and sustain life across the globe.

No specific evidence proves the beginning of Lord Shiva's existence. However, historical records and narratives show that many frustrated kings and individuals adopted Lord Shiva's way of life, finding solace and solutions to their emotional problems. However, it is difficult to identify the first person embodying Lord Shiva's essence. It is clear that such personalities, who embraced the principles of detachment, meditation, and purity, have existed throughout history and played significant roles in addressing and alleviating emotional suffering. The presence and influence of Lord Shiva-like figures across different eras underscore the enduring relevance of these principles in helping individuals navigate their emotional challenges. The earliest acknowledgement of yoga and meditation is historically referred to in India as Lord Shiva's primary personality. The Adi yogi means the first yogi.

Primary records dating back 5000 years ago show that people lived the life of Lord Shiva as a yogic, detached, and meditative lifestyle in the Indian subcontinent and other surrounding regions, which originated from Lord Shiva, the Adiyogi. However, ancient records dating back 5000 years ago show that people lived not exactly, but similar types of detached, meditative, yogic lives in parts of the world other than India, like Ancient Egypt, Sumerians, and Mesopotamians, Indigenous Cultures, and Ancient Greece.

Hence, creation, propagation, and liberation are the psychology of human life not only in India but worldwide, and that is why Hinduism primarily has three deities as symbols of the life cycle.

What it makes us understand is everything is made up of one energy. Through that energy, which means Lord Brahma, humans were created. In humans, those who helped to preserve and propagate human lives are known as Lord Vishnu. When emotional problems arose, some humans discovered purity, stated as Lord Shiva. This only clarifies that all the Trimurti have equal weight in our lives. None is more powerful, and none is less powerful. They are created from a single energy but have been divided into three forms so humans can understand life's real essence. They hold different roles in the cosmos for the greater good, coming from a single energy.

This is adequately explained in the Bhagavad gita quote in chapter 10, verse *20 - "I am the Self, O Gudakesha, seated in the hearts of all creatures. I am the beginning, the middle, and the end of all beings."*

The Trimurti represents the ultimate truth of human life, which I will explore in greater detail in this book. These aspects are fundamental to understanding why Hinduism, the Sanatana Dharma—the earliest of world religions—features three symbolic main deities. As it is said, Hinduism, the Sanatana Dharma, is not merely a religion but a way of life. These three main deities serve as symbols to guide us in embracing the path of life we should follow.

You will understand it more clearly in the further chapters of the book.

CHAPTER 2

The Better Half of Trimurtis

We have understood the Trimurti aspects of life until now, but their better half makes them complete. Now, we will understand the concept of a better half, which merges life's masculine and feminine aspects. Maybe it is more than just theoretical. It is a philosophical living reality within each individual, where the two energy forces, masculine and feminine, exist in every individual, creating a holistic and psychological balance. We will try to understand some of this wisdom from the following Bhagavad Gita quotes.

Bhagavad Gita
1. *Chapter 6, verses 29, 30: The yogi sees all beings existing in me, and he sees me existing in all beings; they see all with equal vision. A yogi who sees me everywhere and sees everything in me never loses me, nor do I lose them.*
2. *Chapter 10, verse 38 - I am death that carries off all things, and I am the source of things that are yet*

to be born. I am fame, prosperity, speech, memory,
intelligence, faithfulness, and patience among women.

The wisdom conveyed in the Bhagavad Gita clarifies that God resides in everything, and everything resides in God, encompassing both masculine and feminine aspects. This teaching suggests that masculine and feminine energies exist within every individual, regardless of gender. Let us explore this idea philosophically.

Knowing about the better half is not something you need to seek out but something to discover from the inside. According to science, the very first species didn't have females and males as two distinct species but the ones who had both the feminine and masculine energy power in them. Then, it was divided into two individual species for the greater good. Hence, the very base of our existence, the male and female, were not different species but some different qualities each individual had to create the balance in life and the evolution of life.

If masculine completes feminine and the feminine completes masculine, it's not because they are incomplete without each other but rather the lack of understanding they have about each other. It's not the opposite things that join you externally and make your life happy. But instead, they evoke something within you internally that makes you happy. It's not the void that you fill. But it's the discovery that you make in yourself. If it's a discovery, why not try to discover it yourself? Maybe by this, you will be independently complete. Then, instead of finding a missing part of yours, you will find the building part for you.

It's maybe not about two incompletes meeting each other to complete each other. Instead, the two complete meetings with each other to greet, build, and support each other. Who knows what is complete and what is incomplete? There may be something incomplete in completeness and something complete in incompleteness. We live in an infinite universe, and it's wise to understand that we cannot reach completeness in our lives, and if we believe we are complete, it makes us complete where we are today. It's the acceptance that makes one complete and the denial that makes one incomplete.

Acceptance is the first step in acknowledging a weakness, and denial is the first step in accepting the weakness. When you accept the flaw, you become ready to overcome it. When you deny your flaw, you are not prepared to change yourself.

In the following text, we will explore each individual's masculine and feminine side regardless of gender through understanding Trimurti and their better half. This will also give the wisdom of balancing feminine and masculine energies within each individual to help them understand and embrace the beautiful life.

Let's understand the completeness in oneself through the wisdom of the better half of Trimurti.

2.1 Maa Saraswati

"Any action cannot be successful without wisdom; creation cannot be created without logic; art cannot be described without the artist; knowledge cannot be gained without experience, and I cannot be described without you. But are you and I different? Yes, we are, and that's where the ultimate fun begins when two individuals meet each other and work on a single agenda in their lives."

Maa Saraswati is the goddess of arts, knowledge, and wisdom, and is a perfect match for Lord Brahma, the creator. Because to create things, you need knowledge. Lord Brahma was the masculine energy that made things, and Maa Saraswati was the feminine energy that helped Lord Brahma with the creation. Let's embrace this in detail.

It took millions of years to form an intelligent human. Nature's significance shows us that feminine energy is all creativity, arts, knowledge, and wisdom, and masculine energy is strength, courage, and power. Philosophically, the central part of Lord Brahma's spiritual energy is feminine, which means Maa Saraswati, and the central part of material energy will be considered masculine.

Many texts, including the Bhagavad Gita, state that spiritual energy is infallible, omnipresent, and omniscient worldwide. We, the material energy, can consciously take part in the evolution of the world, guided by spiritual energy.

Spiritual energy is omnipresent and omniscient because as we get into our spiritual form, it joins the eternity of our existence. They are not attached to earthly material elements, so their existence becomes multi-dimensional.

This is again explained in the Bhagavad Gita Chapter 13, verses 14-15, which we have known earlier in the chapter. It is also described in chapter 10, verse 38. I am fame, prosperity, speech, memory, intelligence, faithfulness, and patience among women. It gives a clear idea about feminine energy.

The dance between masculine and feminine energies shapes the world. The spiritual force of knowledge, wisdom, and art, embodied by Maa Saraswati, is derived from material experiences. Significant wisdom is accumulated through learning from mistakes, overcoming challenges, and applying the correct insights from material life experiences. Spiritual energies then utilise this wisdom to mould both ourselves and our surroundings.

There is little masculine in feminine and feminine in masculine. The masculine and feminine energies of Lord Brahma and Maa Saraswati are the same, but looking at them differently makes us understand them clearly. This mystical unknown cycle also teaches us that the masculine needs to embrace the feminine and the feminine needs to embrace the masculine for the evolution of the world. Then why can one not evolve one's life while balancing them in their inner world?

This is the base of our existence's masculine and feminine energies. This clearly defines their distinction and helps us understand that every aspect carries masculine and feminine forces. It's that, in some parts, the ratio of feminine energy is more. In some, the masculine energy is more, and in whatever we see, whichever side is more overpowering is acknowledged as particularly masculine or feminine.

The beginning of masculine and feminine energies makes us understand the importance of understanding the feminine in masculine and masculine in feminine aspects of life. Balancing them correctly can make any aspect of life smooth and balanced.

Life's ultimate joy lies in discovering unknown, blissful aspects within ourselves. It's truly remarkable when a male who profoundly understands the masculine side of the world begins to embrace and explore the feminine aspects. Connecting with these newfound feminine emotions allows a more profound and comprehensive understanding of the world. Similarly, when a female, well-versed in the feminine side, starts to embrace and understand the masculine aspects, connecting with and discovering the emotions associated with masculinity can also lead to a richer and more complete understanding of the world.

This wisdom is about understanding how one can balance all the aspects of life by introspecting the feminine and masculine energies in the things that one delves into in daily life. Dancing and balancing with these energies can easily give life solutions. It is necessary to balance, but before balancing, it is also essential to understand because balancing will be a masculine thing. However, before that, understanding how to balance things will be the feminine thing to embrace first. To understand Lord Brahma's action and cause, you must embrace Maa Saraswati's knowledge and wisdom through a little observation and gaining as much knowledge as possible about life. To understand these masculine and feminine energies more clearly, let us proceed with Maa Laxmi and Maa Sakthi.

2.2 Maa Laxmi

"No fight can be won without loving the reason behind the fight. No love can be built without the contribution of sacrifice. No house can be built without the materials. The sky can only be seen if you are comfortably standing on the ground. Your inner love and affection can only be expressed and known to the world if you have someone to express it. Then why not for yourself?"

Maa Laxmi is the goddess of wealth. This feminine energy perfectly matches the masculine energy of Lord

Vishnu because to preserve and propagate, one needs a good amount of wealth.

Maa Laxmi is the feminine energy of wealth. Still, Maa Laxmi's role is more significant than just wealth because a good amount of wealth can act as an enemy for a person who doesn't have any purpose in their life. So Maa Laxmi is the feminine energy of the purpose for which the individual earns money to fulfil it.

Whoever was the Lord Vishnu of the world preserved and propagated their civilisation because they seemed to embrace this as their purpose in life. They used their ability to earn wealth and power to fulfil that purpose, which was the feminine energy Maa Laxmi.

And if a woman does it, she will be called the Lord Vishnu. The symbol of Lord Vishnu goes beyond the gender distinction. It is not related to gender but is associated with the quality of love to embrace and save humanity. Here, the woman will be called Lord Vishnu because she shows her masculine side by participating in the fight. The love for which she is fighting and gathering wealth to win the battle. That purpose will be called Maa Laxmi, the feminine side in her.

Visualise Lord Vishnu's job of preservation and propagation as fertile soil that is suitable for the growth of a plant. And Maa Laxmi's purpose behind earning wealth as the seed you will sow in that fertile soil. The more purpose of utility the seed will carry for the evolution of the world, the more profound the growth of plants grown on the fertile soil will be. Each aspect is incomplete without the other. In this example, the plant contributes to preserving and propagating life. The soil is the masculine energy of Lord Vishnu, which is all about strength, courage, and power. The seed is the feminine energy of Maa Laxmi, which is the purpose, beauty, wealth, art, and intention. Until one doesn't understand the balance of masculine and feminine energies, one may not be able to balance one's life properly and contribute to the world as a wise human.

Lord Vishnu's more masculine side is preserving civilisation from destruction. He carries this out with strength, courage, and patience. Still, the reason for which he does this is Maa Laxmi, which means the love of the civilisation they were brought up in. The love for the people they have in their minds and the care built about them in their minds clarify Lord Vishnu and Maa Laxmi's role in our individuals.

Let's take the example of Lord Rama and Maa Sita— the grand epic of Ramayana. Lord Rama, the great avatar of Lord Vishnu, wouldn't have been in history shown as the perfect man, the avatar of Lord Vishnu, if Ramayana hadn't happened. Lord Rama was a man of righteousness. In the epic of Ramayana, Lord Rama was a perfect man who had unconditional love for his wife, Maa Sita. For some internal family issues, they went for vanavas to stay in the forest for 14 years.

When Lord Rama went with his brother and wife to stay in the jungle, Maa Sita didn't carry any wealth with her. This clarifies the understanding that wealth is not what Maa Laxmi is all about. Here, we will see both the masculine and feminine sides of Lord Rama and Maa Sita.

When Ravana kidnaps Maa Sita and takes her to Sri Lanka along with him, does Lord Rama, in that moment, have any wealth? No, right? But then he got the purpose of gathering wealth and power because he needed to save his wife, and for that, he needed wealth to find her and to fight with the person who had kidnapped Maa Sita. Hence, the masculine energy of courage and strength of Lord Rama sought wealth because he needed to save his wife, which was the feminine energy of love, care, and happiness in his life. And then Maa Sita, the feminine energy of love and care for her husband, needed to embrace the masculine energy in her life of courage and strength to wait for Lord Rama while fighting with Ravana. Here, we understand that it was Lord Rama's feminine energy of love and care for his wife. He gathered wealth and an army. Maa Sita embraced her masculine energy of courage and strength to fight with Ravana while waiting for her husband. This shows one needs to evoke feminine and masculine forces in them according to the situations in life.

This story correctly explains to us the role of Lord Vishnu and Maa Laxmi in our individual lives, as the males carry more of the masculine side in them. Females carry more of the feminine side in them, and that is how Lord Brahma has divided us for the greater good. Still, it's essential to understand that one needs to balance these sides. Many males suffer in their lives because they aren't expressive about their emotions to the people around them. This repression makes them mentally unstable, which leads some of them to turn towards intoxication. Females suffer in fighting and standing up for themselves when someone does wrong to them. As a result, some of them get demoralised to fight for themselves.

It's essential to embrace both sides of you. Females need to adopt a more masculine side. Males need to adopt more of a feminine side to understand the nature of life. Balancing this will help any individual have a happy life.

This is the grand epic of a great life. What matters is the dance between the masculine and feminine energies you have within yourself—playing it with the surroundings and displaying whichever side is required according to the situations of life to ace and embrace the real essence of life.

What is in men that women don't have, and what is in women that men don't have except the biological factor that makes their lives difficult to be with each other? I guess it's understanding of each other's feelings. The day you know the value of the other side of the coin is the day when the value of your coin will double, and you will use that coin wisely.

2.3 Maa Sakthi

"The flow is useless without direction. Power needs a purpose to be displayed. Energy needs an object to define its energy. To be positive, one needs a clear idea of the negative. To detach from things, you first need to attach to them. If you don't know what disgrace is, how can you truly understand the absolute bliss of grace? When things become chaotic on the outside, you seek the solution deep within the inside."

Maa Sakthi is the goddess of power, perfectly matching Lord Shiva's detached life. The most powerful thing a human can do is detach from worldly desires and attachments. It is said that having wealth is powerful, but sometimes, rejecting wealth for the greater good is more powerful. So, the act of detachment needs shakti, which means the power to do that.

So, in this case, Lord Shiva's masculine energy of courage and strength to embrace a detached way of life needs the feminine energy of purity, love, and compassion for their ethics and the people around them.

Maa Sakthi symbolises sacrificing outer life passions to evoke inner life goodness. The most powerful thing one can do in this material life is sacrifice the material aspects and desires of life and detach from the happiness formed by material life. These things need more power to do in one's life.

Here, the Lord Shiva is using his masculine power of courage and strength to embrace and nurture the feminine side of love and purpose. To choose the pure and divine way of life. This makes us understand that when in life, you encounter emotional forces of evil that are not humans, but your own emotions and feelings, embracing Lord Shiva's way while using the courage of Maa Sakthi as the power to embrace that way, is maybe the ultimate solution. This ultimately means just detaching from the material aspect of life, which causes those negative emotions to rise in you.

We will get a better understanding when we see the commonly known story of Lord Shiva and Maa Parvati. Lord Shiva is an all-powerful masculine energy who chooses to live a straightforward yogic ascetic life on Mount Kailash to nurture his feminine side, loving the detached, blissful way of life. Maa Sakthi was the wealthy princess of the Himalayan mountains who fell in love with Lord Shiva and his detached way of life. She used her masculine side of courage to sacrifice her wealthy lifestyle to prove her feminine side of love with such a life. This also helps us understand that without the sacrifice of Maa Parvati, Lord Shiva's way of life would not have been addressed the way it was. It gained more value when the princess of the Himalayas showed the world the meaning of a truly happy life.

Detachment is not a sacrifice of the outer world but a greater attachment to inner purity to enrich and excel in real independent happiness. Loving outer things can make you sad one day, but loving yourself internally will not. Attachments to outer people may hurt you. However, attaching to your inner self will never hurt you because people can deceive you, but you will never hurt yourself.

It is not because of your courage that you love things. But because you love things, you become courageous enough to embrace them. You will understand how much you value your feminine side of true love in whatever purpose you will build for life. It will be known by the amount of masculine side of courage you show to embrace and nurture what you love. The road that you think leads to the purpose of life should be understood. The purpose is not the final destination but a companion of your life to achieve all the love you deserve when you walk with your purpose throughout your life. How you seem to sacrifice things is not a sacrifice but giving up everything to reach what you are meant for. You may or may not be courageous by nature. You automatically become courageous once you find your real purpose as a companion.

Getting in touch with Lord Shiva, the pure soul, which is beyond the material aspect of life, is not a destination. It's a way of life, and using Sakthi means the power to walk on that road, which you do because you love that way of life.

The way of one's life is the road of a steep mountain. It's not only about building a masculine side of courage and strength to live a happy, smooth, and prosperous life. Instead, one needs to find the feminine side of what they love to embrace in their journey so that the masculine side of courage and strength will automatically be your companion. Before finding the roads and the strength to walk on them, it's essential to find the loving purpose behind walking on those roads. It's only then that you automatically build the courage to rise no matter how many times you fall on those roads.

2.4 Conclusion

"To feel strength, one must hate weakness. To be courageous, one must deny weakness. And to be loved, one must detach from weakness."

Don't force yourself to merge with anything just because it is how it is, and you should follow what it is blindly. Do not let your weakness choose your life companion because weakness finds comfort. Comfort is not wrong, but getting out of comfort is very difficult. Whatever one thinks their life is all about, everybody needs a companion in life, not as a person but as a purpose. In today's world, any person can leave you anytime, which can demotivate you, but the purpose will never leave. It will always be with you. Choose a life partner who supports and loves your purpose because love for a human may fade away, but real love for a purpose may not.

It's not a single-purpose life but rather a multipurpose one. One doesn't have a single purpose to prove in one's life. There is purpose in many things like family, relationships, friends, work, society, country, colleagues, and many more, and reaching the ultimate objective purpose of life while balancing all this.

Life purpose doesn't mean achieving something extraordinary but doing something very ordinary in a remarkable way. It's not about whom you love, but how you love defines your love.

The Trimurti's love for their purpose showed their ultimate partners in life. Life is not about two individuals coming together but rather two individuals loving the same thing in life, and because of this, they are ultimately loving and staying together. In such an aspect, love can never fade away. It's not always that your life partner should have the same goals as you have, but they should at least have love and respect for your goal in life and you for theirs. Nothing is more important than support in this world. Support is not the strength one feels, but rather the safety one feels. It's not about how someone is helping you to rise. It is always about who is ready to catch you when you are falling. If one has proper backing and support, they can go against the whole world.

It's not about what things men can do but what women can't do and what things women can do that men can't. It's never about equality in the outer world but about making equality of masculine and feminine energies in your inner world. The more appropriately you balance these energies in your inner life, the more you understand their job in the outer world. It is about men learning certain things that make women's lives beautiful even after so many biological struggles. Women learn things that make men brave even after facing many societal failures. You cannot understand someone until you can build empathy for another person.

Balancing masculine and feminine energies inside can make your life easier to understand. Not one particular energy is running the world. Both masculine and feminine energies contribute equally to running and balancing the outer world. In the same way, you can make your inner world happy and enlightened if you balance both of these energies.

CHAPTER 3

Trimurti is the Symbol of Body, Mind, and Soul

Now, we will understand why the Trimurti carries explicitly the symbols of body, mind, and soul. While I will address Trimurti as body, mind, and soul, I will address them, including their better half. Everything has both the masculine and feminine aspects in them.

Before starting, let's understand why Trimurti carries a specific symbol. The first creation of the spices and intelligent humans was only done by the Lord Brahma, so the body became the symbol of Lord Brahma when intelligent humans were created. Then, they built a psychology of living and preserving life, which builds a mind. Hence, the mind is the symbol of Lord Vishnu. When human life became something more than survival and happy living, people faced emotional problems. Thus, humans then found a connection with the soul, the ultimate purity, and the human who did that was called Lord Shiva because they connected to the auspicious pure soul, which is called Shiva in the earliest languages in the world, so Lord Shiva became the symbol of the soul.

This is the ultimate truth of human evolution. Every human, regardless of their birthplace, will inevitably encounter these three aspects of the Trimurti in life. It is a universal truth that each life will face.

Truth is not merely a statement or a hearing. Truth is the profound feeling that one experiences in life. Words may deceive, but feelings are always honest. It's the depth of feeling that can either uplift or shatter you. Sometimes, it's beyond your control to feel a certain way. However, you always have the power to choose your path in life. So, why not choose the path of joy and fulfilment over disgrace.

3.1 Lord Brahma is the Symbol of the Body

"What makes acceptance a weakness and denial a strength, and when does acceptance become courage and denial become vulnerability? When you accept fate and deny faith, you become weak and vulnerable. When you deny fate and accept faith, you become strong and courageous."

Until now, everybody has known that until intelligent species were developed that could preserve and propagate their lives properly and wisely, the Lord Brahma was only present to do the ultimate work of evolution. No one can be 100% sure how exactly the Lord Brahma's spiritual energy works.

No one knows the ultimate truth and purpose behind your birth. Why are you born the way you are born, and where you are born? In the beginning, it is very fortunate and easy for the people who are born fit and into wealthy families, and unfortunate and problematic for the people who are maybe unfit or born into low-income families. Most people make assumptions that they got such birth because of their past life sin, which I'm afraid I have to disagree with. No one is born evil by birth, and your surroundings shape your mind. If one thinks Lord Brahma gave them such birth to punish them, it could be the wrong perspective. Then why did Lord Brahma give them the multidimensional life of humans? The most privileged life on Earth. If you compare it to others, Lord Brahma can provide them with the life of insects.

Everybody's ultimate truth is that they are part of Lord Brahma's energy, and we have reached this evolution through learning from our mistakes and collecting correct wisdom from them. Our life is one in which we can learn something and contribute something significant to the world and the evolution of life, and that's what our history teaches us. Scientifically, the mind chemicals that keep one happy are nowhere related to life privileges and outer appearance. Yes, sometimes it might haunt you to wonder why you didn't have a privileged life. But trust me, that haunt converts into something extraordinary.

It is understood by the feeling you get when you achieve something remarkable in life with your hard work.

Assume there was a poor man who worked very hard in his life, and then his hard work pays off, and he owns a big sea-facing bungalow in a reputed city of the world and has a son. So now imagine yourself as the poor man who has achieved all these things in life and goes to the balcony of his bungalow to drink tea while looking at all the scenery. Imagine the level of happiness you will feel. Now imagine yourself as his son going to the balcony to drink tea. Imagine his level of happiness. It's not very exciting, right? He might not feel happy either because it's a regular thing. It's essential to understand that it's more impressive to think you are worth it than just feeling lucky.

The worth of your life is not decided by luck. Worth is something that is truly yours. The amount of happiness a worthy moment can give is ten times more than the happiness the lucky moments of a whole life can provide. It's not luck that will be counted in your life. It is worth that will be counted. An underprivileged life is a chance to be worthy and be something remarkable in this world.

No one can deny that people who are primarily from unprivileged backgrounds or maybe have privileged backgrounds but live unprivileged lives are more courageous than the privileged and lucky ones to live and hustle in this world. This concludes that you may have performed something brave in your last birth. Because of that bravery, you might have had a more challenging task in this birth. To show the world how to achieve good heights even after such an unprivileged life. And believe me, no one's life is privileged, and everyone understands it at a particular moment. It is just that everybody has privileges and flaws in a specific part of their life. Sometimes, we compare our flaws with someone else's privileges, but we should understand that everybody is not blessed with everything. Everybody has their devils. Their levels might differ, but no one's life is perfect. And the ultimate fun is about excelling in the unprivileged sides of life, which you do if you stand for yourself to fight for yourself. Those are the ones I was talking about in the first sentence; people primarily from unprivileged backgrounds are more courageous because your unprivileged aspect shows you its worth of having it, and that's why when you jump into it to fight with it, you excel in it. The most common examples of those not naturally gifted with good bodies are the ones who primarily excel in fitness because they know its worth.

In an ocean full of uncertainties, one can have the courage to fight all the uncertainties when one understands one's role in what one can do in life and what is in one's hands, following which one may reach the purpose of life. Life's purpose is not always about achieving what you are good at but rather something incomplete in you that you need to accept, overcome, and learn from to help others suffering from it. Doing so will give purpose to your birth and many lives, which you will help.

Body size and bank wealth do not determine a person's greatness. It is determined by how many minds you inhabit with wisdom and how you assist them in overcoming life's hurdles.

If you see people don't pray to Lord Brahma as much as they pray to Lord Vishnu and Lord Shiva, there are many stories about it. I do not disrespect any of those stories. But I do not believe in them, and most of the stories, I think, are like Chinese whisper games. Because if you read the primary scriptures and Bhagavad Gita, you will understand that it is said that Lord Brahma is the ultimate truth, omniscient, and omnipresent. I think Lord Brahma is not praised because of the uncertainties of life and nature. Sometimes, nature is imbalanced; people do not get what they want, not all people are appropriately born, and not all good people get to live for a long time. Nature doesn't always stay supported, and much more reason shows that Lord Brahma, the ultimate truth, is not always fair to everybody, and we may not understand the reasons behind it. This is the main reason that may have stayed hidden, which gives the reason why Lord Brahma is not praised.

What one can do is accept. The first step in solving anything is understanding and accepting that there is a problem. What can we do rather than accept our reality and the ultimate truth? Nothing, right? And what can we do? We are already doing it. So what's the benefit in keeping the rage for Lord Brahma (God) for what he has given you? It will only build negative aspects in your life, eventually hurting you and the ones you love. The only thing we can do is accept the things in our hands.

When one accepts one's reality and the ultimate truth about oneself, one may find ways to develop oneself with a calm mind. If one's mind is constantly arguing in a rage about certain things that happened in one's life without one's own mistake, it can make one stuck in the loop of negativity. It's only when you accept that some things are not in your hands that you become free to progress in other aspects that are in your hands.

What is in hand and what is not is not decided by the things that happened or are no longer in your hands, but by focusing on things and giving 100% on what you can do in the present and future.

Lord Brahma is great and the ultimate truth. But one should understand that you are a part of him, and forgiving Lord Brahma for the uncertainties he has given you makes you great like him. Trusting in Brahma gives you the power to believe that no matter what is lost, there is something greater waiting for you in the future. The heights of your success are not counted by the position you hold but by the depths from where you have reached that position in your life.

Most people are put into difficult situations because Lord Brahma also needs a solution. Brahma puts those individuals in those situations because he trusts that they have the power to emerge from them and inspire the world with their actions and courage.

You will only feel the higher utility of happiness when you know the depths of sadness. Until there is no negative, the positive will not be admired as positive. It's a journey of understanding. One can't understand the value of happiness and goodness until they have seen and felt sadness and disgrace.

One's appearance and luck don't make them valuable in people's eyes. Instead, the hardship, struggle, dedication, and overcoming difficulties in one's life make them valuable, and it's more privileged to be valuable than lucky.

Accept the gift of birth given to you in whichever body form and place you are born, in whatever conditions. Maybe that is the ultimate truth of your life because it's given to you by Lord Brahma, the ultimate truth. And keep yourself physically fit because when you are physically fit, you can embrace a good mind and mental awareness, which is Lord Vishnu.

3.2 Lord Vishnu, the Symbol of the Mind

"One in many and many in one, then who is the one, and who are the many? One is the wisdom, and many are the followers."

Before understanding why Lord Vishnu symbolises the mind, I want to share one psychological fact. When you are born, you don't have a mind. You are born with a body and brain with some neurological abilities. The brain is like the hardware of a computer, and your mind is installed through memories as software after your birth. Up to a certain age, your mind is built by your parents and elderly people in your family, and according to your surroundings, you develop your mind. Most memories in your mind that shape your life already exist in the world and will continue to exist after you. The mind is about acquiring the wisdom and knowledge of prior wise minds and good ways of life to shape your own life, build a good life, and inspire life. It is clearly explained in the following quote-

Bhagavad Gita Chapter 3, verse 21 - Actions of the great humans are followed by the world. The standards they set are emulated by the world.

It simply makes you understand that whatever wisdom your mind carries about life is the wisdom of the people who hold the position of Lord Vishnu in their life. They may be someone from your family, a religious leader, a teacher, a social worker, or an ancient king who fought for humanity. Because your mind holds this wisdom, it helps you in your daily life. It makes Lord Vishnu the symbol of the mind.

So basically, whatever knowledge you have in your mind about living a way of life is the wisdom of your surroundings. People who fought and served good lives and values helped people live happy lives. Their insight, in your mind, ultimately guides you to live a wise, smooth, and happy life. Some significant influence on people's lives comes from those no longer alive. A basic typical example of this is holy books. God hasn't directly written any sacred book but is written by people with god-like personalities who preserved and propagated the world, Lord Vishnus of the world. Any individual who has selflessly contributed to the world is the representative of Lord Vishnu. Lord Vishnu's work preserves life and propagates new ideas into the world so that people can live happily. Sometimes, Lord Vishnu needs to fight with previous laws made by Lord Vishnu because of the loopholes evil minds remove from them and use for their benefit.

Rules are not meant to imprison you or restrict your life because something is not allowed according to the rules. Rules are meant for your freedom and safety when exploring the world. When rules need to change with a concept of sanity behind them, one should rise to change things up.

In Hinduism, Lord Vishnu takes avatars to destroy devils, not because they are born as devils, but because of their weak and evil surroundings. The teachings in their minds made them devils. When Lord Vishnu defeats a devil, he doesn't just beat the devil itself but also the wicked teachings of the devil, preventing them from being carried forward in society. This allows for the propagation of new, positive wisdom until someone misuses it, and another avatar of Vishnu destroys the negative influence and introduces new, positive propagations in life.

These were about prominent personalities. But every individual who consciously puts effort into improving the lives of others, even if they do it for just one person, embodies Lord Vishnu. Their good deeds get installed in another person's mind, which will help the other person, creating a chain of positive influence. Understanding Lord Vishnu in your life will help you know why you are the way you are. Identifying who most reflects your personality helps a lot in understanding yourself.

Be the best Lord Vishnu of your life by understanding the previous Vishnus of your society. The more knowledge and wisdom you carry in your mind, the stronger Vishnu you can become in your life. The more you understand them, the wiser you will become, and the better you will understand how to live your life.

Contribution to the world is essential. Knowingly or unknowingly, every individual contributes to the evolution of life. If you become evil, you contribute wisdom to the world about what one should not do in life. When you become Vishnu, you provide a good understanding that will be carried forward by others in their lives. The contribution amount doesn't matter. What matters is the conscious effort to spread goodness around you.

For example, if there is a cancer patient in your society and everybody is making a contribution to save the patient according to their capacity, and security guards and sweepers giving a little contribution, whoever is receiving help. Will they complain about a small contribution? Will people judge the amount contributed by the security guards and sweepers? No, right. Every contribution will receive gratitude. The same goes for contributing to life evolution. The amount of contribution doesn't matter. Rather, the selfless intention behind it matters.

It's just mesmerising that when you give sound wisdom to the world, even if you die, you stay in people's minds in the form of memory. Don't you think your memory should encourage the coming generation to live a happy and wise life and become the Lord Vishnu of their life?

It's always about adding and upgrading rather than subtracting and missing things in your life. One is born without a mind. Memory shapes the mind. You are what your mind is. Your whole existence is reflected in your mind. Your achievements provide inner rewards and real happiness according to your mind. Therefore, what you achieve is also not entirely yours—some pieces of it already exist. You are simply adding a different experience for the next generation. Living in people's minds, even after we are gone, is truly mesmerising. Could this not also be a purpose of life? To live in people's minds so they can lead happy and purposeful lives through you.

What's gone and what's taken, until you can remember and feel what's gone, it's not indeed taken, and what's not taken is not gone. Accepting the truth may hurt, but what is gone in the present is and will be forever within your memories, and some memories live on. They travel from mind to mind, and some may find solutions through them. If your actions are to travel from mind to mind, let them be the cause of solutions and brave living rather than the reason someone quits fighting their problems.

To achieve this, there are two significant things you need to do in life. Keep walking on difficult roads while hustling and battling all the challenges that come your way, and wisely accept and repent for any wrongs you have done. Observing the paths of wisdom correctly and using that wisdom in your life can also help people, and some people may also use that in their life solutions. Continue walking on the path of life. These two actions have the power to impart immense wisdom to future generations.

It's not what you feel inside but what you show outside that will be passed on to future generations. Choose your battles and actions wisely. Some will carry your wisdom in their life, so be the reason for their solutions, not miseries.

3.3 Lord Shiva is the Symbol of the Soul

"What is outside that is evoked from the inside, and what is inside that is understood from the outside? Attachments, first to material aspects because of inner desires, and then to the inner soul because of the outer miseries."

Lord Shiva represents the pure essence of life—not something pure from the outside, but something pure from the inside. Lord Shiva's way of life helps you connect with the pure soul within you, allowing you to become pure and refreshed. Detaching from the feelings and emotions formed by material aspects of life to transcend real inner connection is the main reason Lord Shiva is the symbol of the soul, and that is the main reason Lord Shiva is also considered as the lord of the devils because people with demonic behaviours also have souls.

"Bhagavad Gita Chapter 7 Verse 28 - those humans who have destroyed their sins by performing noble deeds without any selfish motives with pure minds, those devotees free from attachments of duality caused by love and hatred, worship me in all ways."

Let's use an example to see how this works. Imagine a small child playing in the mud. The child gets covered in dirt and mud. While the mud is on the child, they appear dirty. However, the child is not truly dirty. The outer layer of mud makes them look messy. The child appears clean and beautiful once the dirt is washed away. Similarly, when you wear clothes for a while, they become dirty due to external exposure, but washing them makes them neat and clean once more.

The same principle applies to connecting with Lord Shiva through embracing his way of life. Your soul is inherently pure, regardless of the negative emotions and feelings that may accumulate in your body and mind. Just as washing away dirt cleans clothes, embracing Lord Shiva's way can help you cleanse the negative aspects and restore your inner purity.

Regardless of what humans achieve, finding peace of mind becomes essential at some point. Many people recognise the importance of peace of mind when they need it. Often, they choose to detach themselves temporarily from their current life and visit naturally enriched places. This demonstrates whether or not one is familiar with Lord Shiva's way of life. People instinctively understand that detachment helps them overcome stressful emotions and feelings caused by the day-to-day struggles of material life.

When you embrace Lord Shiva's way, you understand that the stress you experience is not truly yours and is merely a finite existence. Even if your life is not entirely yours, you are here for the experience and contribution. Whether you are feeling extreme difficulties today or experiencing moments of happiness when something good happens, both are of a similar transient nature. Connecting with Lord Shiva provides a sense of solace, helping you realise that the pain you feel through your emotions is not worth clinging to. The more you hold onto it, the more it can lead to significant problems. However, allowing it to flow can help you trace it back to its primary cause, helping you understand its real purpose.

Regardless of your problems, if you look beyond your mental limitations and into your spiritual existence, there is always something new to learn spiritually from every mental challenge.

Who decides what is wrong and what is right? Even right and wrong can't be defined without each other. If there was no wrong, how would we have known what is right, and if there was no right, how would we know what's wrong? Maybe we cannot even prove which term came first in this world, whether it was right or wrong, or whether they existed together by understanding current situations. The only truth of life is the feelings and emotions you feel in your mind through the analysis of the words you speak to yourself.

Whatever an Indian feels in his mind through Hindi words, it is the same feeling a French guy must feel through French words. The same goes for different people. It makes us understand that it is not the words or thoughts that should make you feel troubled about yourself, but rather, the actions you put into your life of sanity in the present moment that matter.

The thoughts without the actions are illusions. The words without the actions are assumptions. The action is the only power that strengthens you to be what you want. So don't let your illusions and assumptions shape your actions. Let actions be wise decisions based on your positive outlook on life, which you interface with your surroundings. In the end, the people will not recollect your thoughts and words. Only your actions will be remembered by others because the meaning of words changes from place to place. But the meaning of actions does not. Being bad is bad, and being good is good even if, in some places, good is the word for bad and bad is the word for good.

Let's understand this with a simple example. If, from childhood, you are taught that the red colour is the black colour and the black colour is the red colour. In that case, you like red, and when you go to the normal shop to buy a t-shirt for yourself and the shopkeeper shows you the red t-shirt and black t-shirt, according to him what he thinks is red and black. You tell him to give you the red shirt, and he gives you the red t-shirt, which is the black colour for you, which leads to confusion. The final call you need to make over here is to go and pick up your red t-shirt. The same goes for the actions. Don't let the words of others define the purpose of your actions. Let your actions speak your purpose behind it because no matter what, your actions are louder than anyone's words. Don't let words shape your actions because not everybody wants you to have a good life. Correct actions solve every emotional problem created by words in your mind. If you're having a problem, you are sane enough to know the proper actions. Sometimes, the action of detachment to connect the pure Lord Shiva within you is the ultimate solution for everybody at a certain point in their life. When one detaches, they understand the real attachments they should make to create happiness and goodness in life.

Nothing is needed to connect with the inner soul. No amount of knowledge or wealth can help you do so. Only outer detachment can ultimately lead you to an inner connection with it.

3.4 Conclusion

Trumurti means three idols, which are not just gods but more than that. In Hinduism, we worship idols and believe in many forms of God because we also believe there is a god in every particle of the universe. I think this is because everything is made up of energy.

When we worship an idol, we don't just worship the idol. We worship a particular idol's qualities and try to embrace those qualities in our lives. Instead of just looking at Hindu gods and goddesses as idols, we should look at them as profound symbols they carry about life. When you worship something that also defines its action through symbols, understanding divine qualities becomes much more straightforward.

It's not only that we believe they are gods; we revere them because we think their way of life and qualities were what made them divine. Until we can see the symbol of their qualities, we may not understand the clear message that the divine God wants to give about life. Whether there be an idol to worship or not, each God at least carries a symbol representing a way of living. So, how can one differentiate between a symbol and an idol? After all, the purpose is to give a sane message through it.

Who is a god, and who is not? We cannot find them until we understand their presence inside us. Only when we know the presence of the divine God within us will we appreciate the God outside us with total gratitude. Understanding these three important aspects of life - the body, the mind, and the soul - represented by the Trimurti deities of Hinduism, Sanatana Dharma, the way of life, in the form of idols and symbols, can help you understand inner and outer life. It's not only about worshipping something outside but about caring for what is inside, not just by prayers and rituals but by living a particular way of life.

CHAPTER 4

Importance of Trimurti

The Lord Brahma, Lord Vishnu, and Lord Shiva represent the symbols of body, mind, and soul; they are important and hold equal value in your life. One should embrace Trimurti through physical fitness, mental awareness, and spiritual awakening.

What is a body without fitness?
An invitation to disease.

What is the mind without the awareness?
An invitation to the thieves.

What is life without the connections of the soul?
Invitations to emotional miseries.

Who is the smart mind and fit body, not connected to the soul?
A greedy animal.

Who is the smart mind connected with the soul in the lazy body?

A confused animal.

Who is a fit body connected with the soul without a smart mind?

An innocent animal.

Who is a fit body and a smart mind connected to the soul?

The social animal.

4.1 Physical Fitness

"Denial is the first step that shows your weakness in not facing and overcoming your problems; acceptance is the first step in defying your fate and beginning to work hard towards what you can truly achieve."

You are what you are physically today, the ultimate truth given to you by Lord Brahma. Suppose you are unhappy with what has been given to you and complain about it. Don't you think that instead of just sitting and cursing, you should show Brahma that you will demonstrate what you can do no matter what you have received? Showing that misfortune will not decide your future. Your faith in earning it will. That's life's absolute joy and purpose. To achieve extraordinary things that were not initially gifted to you. These are the actions that will truly count in the remarkable life you will live.

It's incredible to see yourself as a fighter. No matter the results, a fighter will always be a fighter, and it's amazing to fight for yourself and your existence."

Your physical fitness is directly connected to your mental happiness. When you engage in any exercise in a form you enjoy, whether it be going to the gym, practising yoga, walking, jogging, dancing, playing sports, or other activities, certain positive chemicals are released in your brain. These chemicals help keep you happy overall, leading to a healthy and positive mindset.

It's not about being a fitness enthusiast. What matters is making a conscious effort to nurture the gift given by Brahma. The fight's result doesn't determine whether you are a fighter. The moment you decide to fight, regardless of the outcome, defines you as a fighter. One may be unable to measure the happiness one feels in the mind because it's all a game of brain chemicals. The first thing one can do to produce good chemicals in the mind is physical exercise, whichever form suits you the best.

If you are physically unfit, there is a chance that people involved in the fitness industry may exploit your weakness to make money from you. They may sell fraudulent, easy remedies or products claiming to help you achieve fitness quickly without hard work. However, it is essential to understand that fitness is not a destination or goal but a daily routine that one needs to follow according to their capacity. This is how overall well-being is achieved.

To have a good life, physical fitness is the foundation of everything. It's not about how others perceive your physical appearance. It's about how beautifully you care about your appearance according to your capacities. Whether or not your conscious efforts in physical fitness get counted in this journey will bring inner happiness, which truly matters in the end.

Who is fit and who is unfit is not determined by their external appearance but by how they manage themselves internally. Being fit is not something to show off. It is something to feel. The shape of your body doesn't define what you should think about yourself. Instead, your small, conscious efforts to become fit, which cultivate a love for yourself, determine your happiness, and you will slowly start enjoying the fit process.

No matter how much you love someone else, you can only love them because you are who you are, and your physical aspect plays a part. Shouldn't it be you who decides what you are and what you should be, focusing on the things within your control? Indeed, you cannot expect someone else to love you unless you love yourself. You can love yourself by making small contributions whenever possible to become a better version of yourself—not to show others how much better you can get, but to feel love for yourself in the little things that matter for your existence. It's not what you have in your life. What you make from your life decides the quality of your existence.

Existence is not an overnight journey to be made. It's a lifelong tour to be embraced and enjoyed while contributing to little things slowly but steadily to prove the quality of your existence. One doesn't need to be born into a wealthy family to show their quality of life. Only one thing is needed to define the quality of life: your faith in yourself to try every day to become the better version of yourself, not to prove yourself but to love yourself.

4.2 Mental Awareness

"Unfolding yourself in the flow of life is not just going with the flow but balancing yourself in each fold by detaching and embracing the correct perspectives in your perception. This extraordinary life never leads one to a destination. The only remaining option is to walk each step as a remarkable destiny built by you for yourself. People can only show you a product according to their perspective. However, your independent vision should ultimately decide the worth of that product in your life. It is essential to understand that it's only you who truly understand what you really are, and it's essential to be mentally aware of it. Don't give anyone else the authority to decide for your life and make you aware of your reality. Till the time you walk on the roads of sanity, which means you are not hurting anyone

physically or mentally, including yourself. Walk fearlessly with your head held up high in pride of living the ultimate goal of one's life, which is being true to yourself throughout the journey."

The true self of yourself is made by the true people of your life according to the ways of the people they admire, as some who lived a life of Lord Vishnu so that you can lead a very smooth and happy life. Nature's true nature is evergreen, ever-evolving, no matter what. That is the ultimate truth. But sometimes change can bring a lot of stress to people's lives, maybe one is aware of it or not. Everybody has some sense of their understanding of the world. For example, assume your parents had visited another state or country when they were young, and they found that place very horrible. Today, when you decide to go to the same place because it has developed and holds certain credibility, what would be the first thought in the parent's mind? Obviously, that place is not suitable for my child. And maybe they will not allow you to go there because of that. Perhaps some call it a generation gap rather than a generation gap. It seems to be the perspective gap in seeing the same object from different places. What is essential over here is examining the perspectives and then thinking about them. Mental awareness just doesn't come with a single perspective. To be mentally aware, one needs to think from different perspectives.

We commonly live in a family with four people who eat together, sleep together, enjoy together, and spend most of the time together, but do they all have the same mindsets? No, right. When a family needs to make a particular decision, everybody gives their perspective on that specific decision; according to that, the family collectively decides the decision to be made. The same goes for your mental awareness of yourself and your surroundings.

One cannot understand a single thing with a single perspective. If someone wants to understand an individual, is it possible to understand the person only by understanding their attitude when they work in an office? You cannot. It's just one of the many shades a person carries, so one cannot judge one specific attitude about the person. To understand someone 100%, which may not be possible. But to understand one as much as possible, you need to understand that person's whole life. How they stay with family, how they are with friends, how they behave with ordinary people, how they are with their office colleagues, how they manage life troubles, what their past life problems are, what they want to become, and many more things. Then, you may understand the person when you understand all of their perspectives.

It's hard to understand people not because they live multidimensional lives but because most of them don't even know who they are. If they themselves don't know who they are, how are you going to understand them?

That is why one should be mentally aware of oneself 100% while understanding the perspective one is living in one's life to be and become what one is.

Until you are mentally aware of your life and every perspective properly while fitting your perspective according to the priorities of your life purpose, it's difficult to be mentally aware. One can easily understand oneself from one's perspective on life's priorities of purpose and happiness. And if they are not able to understand themselves, anyone who is mentally sharp can use you for their purpose.

If you don't know what really makes you happy and content in your life, then people may sell their idea of happiness to you, making money out of it for themselves.

Assume you are physically energetic and also academically intelligent. But you are not mentally aware of yourself and your surroundings. In such cases, people who are mentally aware of your surroundings can use you for their benefit. May you be nothing more than a fit, intelligent, and energetic person who has been used by someone else to build a privileged life for themselves by using your efforts.

Mental awareness is a companion that guides you to your path's purpose while fulfilling your contentment in the remarkable journey of life.

4.3 Spiritual Awakening

"Let your passion be driven by goodness while ignoring all its attachments."

Spiritual awakening is simply connecting with the pure-spirited soul within you while understanding the essence of a detached life and consciously accepting the pure way of life—which means not hurting anyone physically and mentally, including yourself—which can be the definition of a pure life. It doesn't mean that you should not defend yourself. This birth is a gift. If anyone is trying to hurt you mentally or physically, it's your birthright to protect and fight for yourself.

When you get spiritually awakened by getting in touch with your pure soul, you may start understanding that nothing is more worthy than the sanity of your mind that you carry to achieve serenity in life. Ultimately, there is no particular proven definition of living a spiritual life. It's not something that you need to go to someone for. Maybe people can show you the ways to get into spirituality. However, the ways don't guarantee that you will connect with your soul; the faith behind walking that way decides how it will be.

Like other purposes of life, you can say spiritual awakening is not a destiny but an aspect that you embrace to make your life more blissful and content. There are three modes of human nature: ignorance, passion, and goodness. According to the Bhagavad Geeta, the ultimate goal is achieving the state of goodness. It suggests that ignorant humans live lazy and unhealthy lives. Passionate humans tend to suffer emotional traumas, leading to emotional suffering. The ones who live with goodness live happily. But how can we get there easily? In that process, we can use and balance ignorance and passion to reach goodness. Let's try to understand. One needs to have a passion for something that one really wants in life, so the passion decides the purpose. If one needs to achieve the purpose, one needs to be ignorant of things that are coming their way to achieve it. Until and unless one has reached the passion for carrying it with the attitude of goodness, how can one demand a feeling of goodness when one meets one's purpose in life? Here, we understand the balance. You need to have a passion for your purpose and an attitude of goodness as a companion, and in that process, you need to be ignorant of all the things that are not worth disturbing your journey to feel real goodness.

It's not that a sinner cannot achieve a spiritual awakening in their life. Maybe they will take more time, but it's not impossible. One needs to remember that the essential thing in spiritual awakening is not surrendering to someone else but surrendering to your inner self, understanding your inner self, and connecting with it, which is already connected to the ultimate reality. It doesn't matter how big a sinner you may be. By surrendering to yourself and sacrificing your life in the service of the contribution towards the greater good of underprivileged lives, you can reach a state of spiritual awakening. What matters is the motive and intentions behind that act.

Suppose you are physically fit and energetic and mentally very smart and aware. But if you don't know about spirituality and detachment, you will suffer emotional trims like anger and greed. In that case, someone who knows about spirituality can loot you by giving you some remedies of spirituality that some of the fraud babas do. What is the use of your benefit of being fit and earning so much when you are ultimately going to give that money to some fraud baba, which is just pretending to help you to cope with some ancient Vedic wisdom and pretending to solve your problem?

You cannot divide left and right, up and down in correct proportion until you know the proper centre. Only when you see the centre can you correctly divide and balance all the dimensions. Connecting to your inner-spirited soul by balancing and detaching from material aspects that are confusing you is like embracing the centre of your ultimate dimension, where you can control your multidimensional life. This is what spiritual awakening is. Having an apparent and profound view of your overall life from the very centre of it is what life is all about.

How does one know if they are spiritually connected to their soul, which leads to spiritual awakening? It is when your emotions don't control you, but you control your emotions. This occurs when you understand your life beyond the material aspects. Whatever you are feeling emotionally is all because of the earthly elements that make you think certain things in life, and that is why detachment is taught in almost every religion. The purpose is not to detach from happiness but to understand detachment so that negative emotions shouldn't trouble you. That is why once you master detachment, you will live a life of goodness, leading to spiritual awakening.

It's not that you won't feel anything negative. Rather, you will easily understand how to cope with that feeling when you embrace spiritual awakening by connecting to your inner pure soul.

4.4 Conclusion

If any of these aspects are neglected, your life may become imbalanced. If you embrace all three qualities of life as your companions, then there are very few chances of you suffering for a long time. Because you are physically fit, which means a healthy mind, being mentally aware means knowing how to act in the world, and if anything goes wrong, you already know detachment through which you will solve your problem.

Everybody will encounter the Trimurti trilogy of life at some point because these three aspects are the ultimate truth of life. However lazy you may be, you need to take care of your physical health in the long run. However, if you are mentally unaware of yourself and your surroundings, life will teach you that it is essential to be mentally aware to get attached and embrace anything in this life. Nothing is permanent, and times come when you need to detach yourself from certain aspects or things in life for your greater good. So, as these aspects will be a part of your life, why don't you consciously try to embrace these things in life, which will 100% gonna make your life better than before.

There is no rocket science behind this. It's just three aspects of life you need to take care of, which will then take care of you. Simply embrace these three aspects of life into your daily life. If you embrace these three qualities, you are 100% going to be ace in your life.

It's not just the psychology of a single life. It's the psychology of human life on Earth. Only humans have the power to consciously embrace it to achieve and live a liberated life of goodness.

CHAPTER 5

Yoga to Embrace Trimurti in Life

India's uniqueness is rooted in our vibrant culture, history, and civilisation. Hinduism, Sanatana Dharma, is not merely a religion but a unique way of life. As we embark on the journey of the Trimurti trilogy, we begin to understand the distinctiveness of this way of life, sparking curiosity and a desire to learn more.

The most unique thing that Indians gave the world was yoga. When you hear about yoga, the images that may appear in your mind may include people doing meditation and different physical postures to achieve unique life fitness goals. But now we will understand the yogas of life, which will be beyond your assumption about it. It's not that yoga is not what you might imagine; instead, its goal is much bigger than that.

5.1 What is the Definition of Yoga? And Its Importance?

Definition: Yoga is a multifaceted discipline encompassing physical, mental, and spiritual practices to achieve harmony and balance in the body, mind, and soul. The word "yoga" is derived from the Sanskrit root "yuj," which means "to yoke" or "to unite." It signifies the union of the individual consciousness with the universal consciousness or the integration of body, mind, and soul.

Yoga is not just a theoretical concept but a practical discipline that brings tangible benefits. The action of the body is strength, the action of the mind through the body is intelligence, and the action created by aligning body, mind, and soul is wisdom. This wisdom is what yoga helps us achieve in our daily lives.

Yoga is also a philosophical system that provides a framework for understanding the nature of existence, the mind, and the path to self-realisation. It is a way of life that encourages mindful living, self-discipline, and a deeper connection with oneself and the world around us.

So until now, whatever you read was a part of ultimate life yoga. The essence explains your material internal connection to the external eternal spiritual existence. Everybody has to know the importance of the connection between body, mind, and soul, and it's essential to understand that one is free to embrace this ultimate yoga of life the way one wants. The ultimate goal is maintaining physical fitness, mental awareness, and spiritual awakening and ultimately making a connection between body, mind, and soul. Living a blissful life while uniting them means achieving the ultimate yoga of life.

However, four main yogas are given in the Vedas to help people understand how to embrace them quickly. Understanding this will give you a clear idea of embracing the connection between body, mind, and soul. Let me explain this yoga in a very simplistic way. One doesn't need to go to some yoga or meditation classes if they don't have time for it. It's not about whether you should go to learn yoga or not. There are some unique yogas for which you genuinely need someone specialised to teach you, but if you don't have that much time in life. If it is not your priority, then you can embrace the ultimate yoga of life by just understanding the four yogas wisely. You can learn by yourself and apply it daily to build and embrace a blissful life.

So, the four main types of yoga are kriya, jnana, karma, and bhakti. If you understand these four yogas wisely, you will understand that they are not just yoga but a way of life. Let's try to understand yoga one by one.

Before explaining this, I am not challenging or disbelieving the traditional form of yoga. I have complete gratitude towards my culture and its traditional ways, which embrace yoga in conventional ways. I am not suggesting that you do or perform any challenging and unique type of body yoga without a proper yoga trainer. I will also not do that. I am giving a different perspective on the four main yogas of Sanatana Dharma so that you can easily follow in your life, which will help you build a good, happy, and blissful liberated life.

5.2 Kriya Yoga

Definition: Kriya Yoga is a spiritual practice that focuses on controlling and harmonising life force energies (prana) within the body to achieve self-realisation and spiritual awakening. The term "Kriya" comes from the Sanskrit root "kri," meaning "action," and "yoga," meaning "union." Thus, Kriya Yoga can be understood as a practice of actions or techniques aimed at achieving union with the divine or higher consciousness.

So kriya means action you perform, and yoga means uniting with your divine consciousness, right? But when we talk about action, its context is the actions that keep you healthy. When you have a healthy body, it becomes easy to connect with the divine, which is the essence behind it.

Actions may seem useless if the results behind those actions are not fulfilled. Even a very correct form of action cannot be 100% useful when one doesn't clearly understand the reason behind the actions. But sometimes, a little effort can also give excellent results if you do it with total understanding.

So, actions can be in any form. The ultimate goal is to keep your body fit and give whole gratitude to the body given to you in any form. How can one imagine connecting with the inner soul if you are not consciously putting effort into keeping the body fit in which that soul resides? It means the actual value of the temple's God is known by its appearance, which is given by people's actions who believe in that God and contribute to the temple's strength, architecture, beauty, and cleanliness. It goes the same with your body. The more you care for it, the more you connect with your soul.

So it's not mandatory to only perform certain kinds of actions that will lead you to connect with your inner self. It is not the actions connecting you to the soul, but the results that actions give help you connect. What are the results? The result is a fit and healthy body both internally and externally. One can achieve that in many ways through various actions one is comfortable doing in one's busy life, like walking, running, jogging, going to the gym, sports, yoga, tai chi, and many more. It's not essential to look fit, but rather feel fit. It's not that one needs to be a pro in what they are doing, but one should be mindful about what they are doing. It's essential to enjoy this process. It's only when you enjoy the process that you do not care about the results, and it's only then that you will continue doing it even if that doesn't give you results. Physical fitness is not a destiny to achieve but a way to walk on.

According to the book's concept, practising Kriya Yoga will help you express gratitude for Lord Brahma's gift by making yourself physically fit. This will also make your mind fit and help build mental awareness, which will help you embrace the next yoga, Jnana Yoga.

5.3 Jnana Yoga

Definition: Jnana Yoga, often called the "Yoga of Knowledge," is a spiritual practice centred on realising one's true nature. It involves a philosophical approach to understanding reality and the self, primarily through self-inquiry, reflection, and the study of spiritual texts. The goal of Jnana Yoga is to transcend ignorance and realise the unity of the individual self (Atman) with the ultimate reality (Brahman).

The definition itself makes it very clear to understand this yoga. It's the knowledge one should have of the self and reality through various studies, including spiritual studies, to unite with the inner soul and the ultimate truth of the Lord Brahma.

Knowledge alone can't be the path to understanding. It also needs wisdom. What is the use of knowledge if one doesn't understand the real reason behind that knowledge? Wisdom is acquired when you use the knowledge practically and then learn from it. It's not the knowledge that helps one achieve good heights in life, but the wisdom to know how and where to apply that knowledge helps achieve things in life.

When one properly understands oneself, one can correctly apply knowledge while possessing sound wisdom. One can only know what kind of knowledge can give them and their life the real essence of wisdom their life holds, and no one can, other than their own self, understand themselves 100%. Some people try to understand others when they don't know themselves. Understanding oneself doesn't take something of extraordinary quality. You need to observe the little things you do consciously.

Sometimes, to seek what is in your inner world, you need to observe what matters in your outer world. And sometimes, to understand the outer world, you need to acknowledge it with your inner wisdom. Who is outside and what is inside is not decided by the things and feelings your outer and inner worlds carry, but the smoothness of the transaction you do between them clarifies what is worth and what is not.

To embrace Jnana Yoga, one should first acquire self-introspection and understanding. Then it's essential to understand your core beliefs, life ideas and concepts, life purpose, religion, society, people of your culture, country, and many more. The more knowledge you acquire, the more you will understand life and its actions. Suppose you have the proper wisdom of life. In that case, only you will mostly take correct actions in life, which will help you run your life smoothly, which means you have attained the essence of Lord Vishnu means mental awareness. And it will be easy to perform the next yoga very wisely, which is Karma Yoga.

5.4 Karma Yoga

Definition—Karma Yoga is one of the four main paths of yoga in Hindu philosophy, emphasising selfless action to achieve spiritual liberation (moksha). The term "Karma" means "action" or "deed," and "Yoga" means "union." Thus, Karma Yoga can be understood as the path of union through action, where one engages in one's duties and responsibilities without attachment to the results.

Karma Yoga is a selfless action done to help others, and it's the highest form of yoga in Sanatana Dharma. It also gives a clear essence to your life. Whatever we have understood in this book ultimately leads to one conclusion: you will contribute to this grand evolution of life, willingly or unwillingly. So, the primary purpose in life is to contribute to this evolution of life, and you can do that by doing Karma Yoga.

So, until now, you might have understood the chronology I have kept while explaining the yogas. First, being fit by doing Kriya Yoga will help you acquire wisdom, which means Jnana Yoga, which will make you wise in your Karma Yoga. Especially in today's world, where there are so many frauds, you need to be aware of your surroundings before helping anyone. It's essential to understand that the first thing you need to help is yourself, your family, and the society you live in.

The results that you acquire after doing Karma Yoga selfless actions are going to be most beneficial for yourself. The selfless actions of karma are not to please anyone outside but to connect with the purity inside. Yes, it is necessary to be physically fit and mentally aware. Still, even if you don't have these two and if you help someone selflessly, your inner conscience will provide serenity, and you can easily connect with the inner soul.

In Karma Yoga, what is given and received are both important. It's about offering your actions with the purity of your soul and understanding that true fulfilment comes from this connection. Giving without expecting anything in return brings you inner bliss and a deeper connection to your soul. In Karma Yoga, the amount you give or how you help is less important; what truly matters is the intention behind your actions.

When you do Karma Yoga, the Lord Brahma's spiritual energy mysteriously helps you with your life problems. It is like exchanging. You're assisting the Lord with building material energy. In return, Brahma helps you with its spiritual power. Many of the readers may have experienced this in their lives. If they had helped someone selflessly, they would have experienced many instances of unknown forces. When you do your Karma Yoga properly and connect with your inner soul, you can passionately do the next Bhakti Yoga.

So here you did the job of being the Lord Vishnu of your life, helping preserve and propagate. Then, you can easily attain spiritual awakening through Bhakti Yoga, ultimately connecting to Lord Shiva.

5.5 Bhakti Yoga

Definition: Bhakti Yoga is dedicating oneself wholly to a personal god or the divine with love, reverence, and devotion. It involves engaging in practices that cultivate a deep, personal relationship with the divine, emphasising the importance of faith and surrender over intellectual knowledge or selfless action.

Some important aspects of Bhakti Yoga are devotion, surrender, love for the divine, and connecting to the inner soul to understand the outer divine.

So, the first thing we will understand here is devotion to God. Giving devotion is like giving gratitude. Giving gratitude to life and the God you believe in is essential. When will you genuinely thank God when things go well in your life? Right. So, the main reason I explained the other three yogas to you before coming to the Bhakti

Yoga is that if you do the above three yogas properly, the maximum chances are that you will lead an extraordinary life without any miracles happening. When everything goes smoothly, you give your wholehearted devotion and gratitude to the God and divine power you believe in.

It's hard to surrender outside when you cannot surrender to things inside; surrendering inside means surrendering to all your bad habits that have taken control of your life. Respect your own life and surrender to all the bad things by yourself because only you understand your reality. When you surrender to your inner truth, you get a clear idea of things you need to surrender to in the outside world. It can be anything that is troubling you or helping you. You must surrender to working hard even if the results are not showing. You also need to surrender to bad habits that are troubling your life by quitting them. Surrendering is about understanding the pros and cons and balancing your life by embracing the pros and avoiding the cons.

Meditation is a key aspect of Bhakti Yoga. It provides clarity and understanding. When you meditate, you gain a clear understanding of your inner self, which in turn helps you understand the actions of the divine energies in your life. It's a process of enlightenment that connects you with your inner soul and the divine forces around you.

These four yogas are theoretical concepts and practical tools that can be applied daily. In four simple steps, let's explore how to incorporate these yogas into our lives.

Understanding and applying these principles can lead to a more balanced and fulfilling life.

5.6 4-Step Daily Life Yoga

Step 1

Kriya Yoga: Mindfully practice physical fitness in any form possible.

"In the great grand journey of life, it's good to have a fuelled and fit body to explore and excel on every road."

People can do anything they think they can to keep themselves physically fit. Physical fitness produces certain positive chemicals in the mind, which keep your mind happy and aware and help you do your particular job mindfully. So, at the start of the day, one should give half an hour to physical fitness, doing it mindfully. With the correct breath work, the only thing to do here is start doing it as per your capacity, and you will automatically increase it when you start getting benefits out of it. Remember, we are doing this not to show fitness but rather to feel fitness.

Step 2

Jnana Yoga: Being aware of your inner self and outer surroundings.

"Every human has the same destination, but the contribution while walking multiple paths is different.

Having the GPS of knowledge with you is necessary to explore these multidimensional ways."

Once your 1st step is achieved, you will be good at correctly introspecting about yourself because you automatically become self-aware when you mindfully practice physical fitness. This will help you put more conscious efforts into understanding your current inner state and can give you clear ideas of how to deal with things in a day. Additionally, one should gather current knowledge of one's surroundings and work through any means possible, such as newspapers, social media, the internet, news channels, and many more. With current knowledge, you will adequately prepare for the day. It will make you mentally aware of the need to take particular actions.

Step 3

Karma Yoga: First, help yourself and then contribute to the surroundings according to your capacity.

"Selflessly helping lost souls in your journey is the secret, sacred door to connecting directly with your inner, pure soul."

When you apply the 2nd step, you become mentally aware of what actions you can take throughout the day. Only when you are mentally aware can you practice Karma Yoga properly. Because through mental awareness, you will understand whom you should help, and charity begins at home. When you and your family are stable, then only you can help the poor and needy, so first help yourself by giving 100% to your work, which pays you. Then, according to your capacity, you should help people around you. It's not necessary to help financially, but you can help anyone with small actions of cheering people, helping old people, giving a bright smile to someone who is looking sad, or giving someone moral support; each act of kindness will contribute to your Karma Yoga, and this will really make you feel good. This will help you connect with your inner purity.

Step 4

Bhakti Yoga: Surrendering and giving gratitude to your inner self to connect with the ultimate spiritual energy.

"The attitude of gratitude can create a never-ending ecstasy of goodness, which wisdom ultimately gives a serene essence to each moment of life one lives."

When you finally follow all three steps, you have the maximum chance of having a smooth and happy day. But things will not always go as planned, no matter how perfectly you do everything. It's good if your whole day goes well so that you will automatically show gratitude for good happenings, which will happen most of the time, not suddenly but after some months when you follow these steps in your daily life. But it's also more important to give gratitude when things go wrong.

Let's see how one can do that. Just calmly sit alone, introspect, and figure out the whole day what and how things happened very sanely; introspect mistakes that you and others have made that have caused the problem. Also, learn from it, forgive yourself and others and never repeat it, give gratitude for making it out, and learn something positive from it; if things were not in your hands, think that it was Lord Brahma's (god) will, and there is something good hidden behind it. Accept it because that is the only thing you can do. When you figure out all these, make a small plan to overcome them and follow it for a few days. Work on it, and repeat these steps daily.

CHAPTER 6

Help from Trimurti

"The one in whole and whole in one? Who is the big, whole, or one? No one rather than the journey which makes you one in whole and whole in one."

In the book, we clearly understand being strong from within and being complete for oneself without external help; that is what life really is: being strong independently.

But it's life. One cannot live alone without anybody's help. We are part of this grand evolution, which you and I are not doing single-handedly but together. We also need the help of other people in life, not as support but to make ourselves stronger independently.

When one takes support, no one can justify who is weak, the person taking support or the person supporting. The person supporting the one in trouble might have gained that wisdom from mistakes, and the person taking help is strong enough to ask for it. In today's world, the most powerful thing one can do is ask for help. Showing your vulnerability does not mean you are too weak to survive. It shows you have a powerful love for yourself and are seeking help to survive. When a person wins something, he's not the only person who wins. Instead, every person who supported that person in their journey wins. Maybe in people's minds, that person's way of life will be there, which will help them to live a particular way of life. However, the person is admired by many and has a place in many minds. Who will be there in his mind, the people who helped them, right? Then who is significant, the person who won or the people who helped them win? In life, no one is won alone. When one mind wins, many minds are behind it.

6.1 Visit Lord Brahma

"The ultimate you exists in this existence of your body, and keeping it fit is the ultimate truth and priority of life."

Lord Brahma, the ultimate truth, represents the body, and we must keep our body fit in whichever way it may be. It is essential to understand the way nature works. No miracles happen in life overnight, especially in the physical aspect. No person can guarantee that you will transform your body overnight. This is the world of science, and everything has proper scientific ways to make things correct. So it is essential to understand that one needs to keep oneself healthy and fit according to science and not follow some fake people who have phoney tantras and mantras. A person with actual knowledge of tantra and mantra will never suggest that bodily problems can be solved magically or overnight.

Taking care of the body first involves visiting people and professionals who know and have studied the body. Don't fall prey to immediate results. Whatever your age is, you have not grown in one day. It has taken a lifetime to reach where you are today. Everything has a proper way to achieve, so proper guidance is the most important thing. Before taking guidance, you should know appropriately from whom you should take help.

To maintain your health, it's crucial to seek advice from certified professionals and go to proper gyms, yoga centres, fitness centres, and many more. If financial constraints are a concern, consider visiting places like public gardens and playgrounds. Engaging in physical activities in these places can also contribute to your well-being. Small conscious efforts like walking can also give significant results, but it's essential to have consistency, enjoy the process mindfully, and make it a part of your routine.

If you find yourself feeling guilty or ashamed when you see a fit person, it's essential to understand that your unfit body doesn't give you guilt, but not putting conscious effort into making yourself fit makes you feel guilty. Sometimes, mental barriers can prevent you from taking action, and that's when seeking help becomes crucial. Remember, seeking help is not a sign of weakness but a brave step towards a healthier you.

Visit all the places that can keep you fit because fitness is an investment that will never turn into a loss.

6.2 Be Friends with Lord Vishnu

"However strong one may be, one cannot alone excel in all the works of life. Friendship is the key to excelling in this grand journey of life, where you exchange wisdom and actions with each other."

First and foremost, it's crucial to befriend knowledge and wisdom, for they are the ultimate companions of your mind. Everything in the world may come and go, but the knowledge and wisdom you hold will never depart. They form the very foundation of all that you perceive in your surroundings.

Be friends with people who serve the world in preserving and propagating lives. People like social workers, police, politicians, teachers, gurus, religious teachers, etc. People who are doing selfless work for other people. It's also important to be wise with whom to be friends because, in these categories, many people are also frauds and can loot you. Still, many individuals are doing selfless work. Being friends with them is very helpful because these people know how the system works, and if you get caught in trouble, they can help you get out of it.

Many of us go to meet such people when we get into problems, and when we do, we might find a big queue of people who need their help. Therefore, would it not be wise to befriend them before you get into a problem? Doing this can also contribute to your help and guidance to some people through them. So, you will also fulfil your duty of contributing to the world's evolution.

Befriending those in positions of authority and power doesn't diminish your worth. On the contrary, it elevates you to their level. It's well known that your value is determined by the company you keep. Therefore, it's wise to surround yourself with good people.

6.3 Find Lord Shiva

"Purity is not measured by visibility but by the vision behind it. It's your vision that objectifies and justifies outer things with your inner reality lens."

Finding Lord Shiva, the pure soul, means finding the purity in every essence of life. Finding Lord Shiva means finding purity within you, which will help you connect with the divine. Especially in spirituality, when searching for God, people follow many difficult paths in their lives. People sacrifice things, adopt specific pure ways, live detached ways of life, follow specific diets, and many people start living very disciplined lives like monks. The ultimate result is one reaches to embrace purity in life, and through that, one connects to the divine.

Before finding God outside, one needs to find purity inside. Only when you find purity in yourself by solving the problems of your material lives that are troubling you, with detachment, you finally learn to understand divine energies.

Many people can selflessly help you on the path, like monks and yogis who understand what connecting to the divine means. Many people have embraced the life of a monk to guide lost souls and provide sanity to their lives, which helps them attain serenity.

The pure and impure are just states of being sane and insane. When you find the meaning of life in sane ways, it keeps you in good health. You then detach from things in life that make you insane about life. Things sane for one may be insane for another, and vice versa. So things don't matter, but what your state of mind thinks is sane and pure is all that matters if it will not hurt anybody physically or mentally, including yourself.

Regardless of the path you choose in life, your inner perception determines your connection to the purity of the outer world. Until our inner reality is aligned with purity, we cannot fully connect with the external world's purity. This understanding empowers us to take control of our spiritual journey.

6.4 Conclusion

"The easiest way to live a strong life is to understand that no way of life is right or wrong until it is sane; it's appropriate to walk on."

This is the best way to excel for a good, happy, and long life. It is the journey of a grand, multi-dimensional life. Your emotions and feelings are your superpowers for the happiness you can feel. Choose to have them wisely. Be strong enough from within; only then will you have the right wisdom to be with wise people.

When you are lost in the darkness of your life, remember to unlock the doors of love from where the light of your loved ones will guide you and illuminate your ways while helping you cross every hurdle of your roads by supporting you.

Visiting Lord Brahma, being friends with Lord Vishnu, and searching for Lord Shiva. It is essential to embrace and excel in the aspect of Lord Brahma, the body; Lord Vishnu, the mind; and Lord Shiva, the soul, which will give you physical fitness, mental awareness, and spiritual awakening, which are the ultimate ways of life.

.

CHAPTER 7

Spiritual Love

My last message in this book is about spiritual love, the best thing I have learned in my psychotic, chaotic journey. Spiritual Love is the world's best feeling, and it's the feeling everyone can experience in their life. It's free, and the best thing is that it gives justice to every life on Earth. It's not something to achieve in life but something to feel for yourself when you express it selflessly.

7.1 Detachment

"Detachment is the first step in creating a real attachment to the serenity in life."

"The serenity of life is like the light that awakens the real spirit within when you detach yourself from the dark shadows of life and get attached to the different shades of light that enlighten your soul."

Life is full of attachments, and it's the way we are designed. Without attachments, life would not have been so evolving and lovely. If there had been no attachments, the world might not have progressed. What is in attachments that hurts and in a detachment that doesn't? It's the value of things that are valuable in your life. If your attachment is troubling you, it's only because you are not getting the same value in return when you are still attached to that person or thing in life. It's your will. Maybe it's tough for you to detach from them, so rather than detaching from them emotionally, we can detach from the outcome we want from them. It's not the attachments that hurt. It's the outcome we expect that hurts. So, rather than detaching from that person, one should detach from the expectations one keeps from that person or thing.

The dance we do to balance detachments and attachments creates ultimate fun. Nothing is permanent in life. Maybe you will detach from those things you are attached to today and attach to those detached. People change, purposes change, places change, you change, nature changes, and everything changes except your soul. You are ultimately attached only to the soul within you, and you are just an instrument being played by these aspects in the grand journey of your soul.

Life is not about detaching from things that don't know your worth. Instead, it's about getting attached to something that does, where you automatically happily detach from things that trouble you. So, to detach from things, you need to attach to something significant and valuable in your life. Nothing is more beneficial than our inner soul; it is the foundation of our existence. Adopting that gives you spiritual happiness, which no external power can destroy.

7.2 Sacrifice

"Sacrifice is the art of displaying your meaning of love."

"No one will be willing to sacrifice things in their life if they don't love anything. Maybe the synonym of love is not 'like'. It's sacrifice. One only happily sacrifices things when one loves the reason behind that sacrifice."

Imagine a low-income family having dinner. The man is the only source of income in that family. He works hard as a labourer, and four people are in the family; out of four, two have finished their dinner, the mother and the elder sister. The younger son is about to finish it, and when the younger son finishes it, being very young, he expresses his feeling that he is hungry and there is no food left. The only food left is of the father. And that father sacrificed that food to his son. Even if he needs that food because he needs to work hard for the family, he chooses to give food to his son. So, does this sacrifice provide him with sadness or real happiness? When would he have seen his son's happy face after giving him the food? Even if he sacrificed, that sacrifice will 100% give him the feeling of happiness.

You do not sacrifice things because you are someone great, but because doing little acts in your daily life for people you genuinely love and care for gives you the feeling of being something great.

Everyone's first sacrifice will be for someone they truly love, and that sacrifice will make you feel worthy enough to do so. So, your sacrifice doesn't show your greatness in life, but the worth you give to the things you love, and it's wise enough to love your life.

7.3 Forgiveness

"Forgiving is forgetting the things that trouble you."

"Forgiveness is the perfect act of letting go of your ego, which only wants to satisfy its anger, keeping what ultimately hurts you."

First, you must forgive yourself for everything you did and are troubling you constantly. One needs to understand that if you do anything wrong, you feel guilty about it. The guilt is proof that you are not a bad person. Guilt is a sign of a person's good conscience. So guilt is the ultimate proof of being a good person, and whatever you did was a mistake. If you feel that you have committed some big mistake, go and confess it and seek forgiveness from wherever you can and need to, but it's essential to forgive yourself until you cannot forgive yourself; you cannot forgive others in your life.

If you have forgiven yourself or someone you love, what is your feeling after that? The very first feeling you feel is maturity. Forgiveness is something that immature people cannot afford in their lives because one needs a very mature mindset to forgive people who have done wrong to them. It's not that one should not fight for oneself, but you should also know that if people have gone on different paths, one should not disturb one's sanity and keep thinking about it.

Forgiveness can remove your mental burdens, giving you a feeling of relief when you accept that act as Lord Brahma's will and let Lord Brahma deal with it.

7.4 Selfless Love

"Love is not attained by embracing it but by selflessly giving it the freedom to be something because of which you love it."

Is love something you want to embrace because it gives you an extraordinary feeling from the inside, or do you want to make them feel special in their lives because you love them? It's both. It is only when something makes you feel extraordinary after seeing or being with them that the extraordinary feeling is expressed through your actions toward them, which makes them feel something special about themselves.

"Don't let your material world decide the act of your real love. Real love is not a finite material thing to own; it's an infinite spiritual journey to feel and explore."

Real love cannot be selfish. It can only be selfless. When ego jumps into your love life, one should understand that you no longer love that person but think you own that person. The most prestigious thing in human life is the freedom to live how they want. What is really in your hands is loving them selflessly. Loving selflessly may not ultimately result in you ending up being with them. But if you love them selflessly, then the person you love may not be with you, but you will always hold love and respect in their mind. What else does a real lover want? If you have made a small place in the person's mind, someone you love is more than enough to justify your love. Being in someone's mind and memories is the same as being in their life. Your selfless love doesn't make you naïve, but it makes you a great person, and the feeling of being great is more than the feeling of being loved.

7.5 Kindness

"Kindness is the greatness you can show through your actions."

"Whatever one becomes in life, reaching extreme heights until one doesn't understand the importance of kindness, one cannot achieve greatness."

One doesn't need to do something extraordinary to be incredible. Small acts of kindness can make you outstanding in people's eyes. Who is great and who is not is not decided by people who rule but rather by who rules in people's minds. Acting with kindness may not help you build a good amount of wealth for yourself. But it can rule the minds of the people you have been kind to. There are two types of rulers in our society: 1st are those people respected because they are feared, and 2nd are the people respected because they are loved. At any time, respect out of love is more significant than respect out of fear.

Being kind is a mighty weapon of greatness that everybody cannot afford to hold. Kindness shows one's level of sanity, which gives people a feeling of serenity in the moment of the act of kindness they receive from you.

Everybody has been kind to someone at some point in their life. What is the first feeling you feel when you are kind? It's the feeling of brotherhood and oneness you think in that moment. It's the most blissful feeling to see the happiness one shows through one's eyes when you act kind to them.

This happiness is the spiritual happiness attained by kindness.

7.6 Spiritual Love

"Loving something beyond existence, where everything ends and starts, which cannot be described in words but whose little presence can give feelings of peace in the darkest moments of life, is spiritual love."

Spiritual Love is something parents do for their children. Spiritual Love is what children do to their parents. Spiritual Love is what brothers and sisters have. Spiritual

Love is something you give to your family. Spiritual love is in the selfless acts you do for the love of your life. Spiritual Love is what best friends have. Spiritual Love is what you have for your mentor and what your mentors have for you. Sometimes spiritual love is one-sidedly loving someone you love and knowing that person will not love you back. Spiritual Love is loving yourself beyond your material existence in life.

All the relations I have mentioned about spiritual love are the aspects of your life you love selflessly without expecting any kind of love in return, and that is why it is pure love beyond material aspects: it is spiritual love.

Spiritual Love is the only place where you can detach for the greater good, love to sacrifice things, forgive so that you can start a new chapter of life, love selflessly to embrace the actual value of love, and act kindly to rule in people's lives in this great grand evolution of life.

"The spiritual life is beyond feelings and emotions, attachments and detachments, love and hate. It's the total freedom of being with your inner self while connecting with the independent goodness of the ultimate reality of the Auspicious universe, which you cannot express but can only feel."

Om Namaha shivaya
Everything to the purity.

Acknowledgements

Firstly, I want to thank my little sister, Mrunal Ashok Bharati Shinde (Gudda), for designing and formatting my book in her busy schedule.

"No problem in this world can be greater than your willpower to overcome it. This is the primary teaching I learned from my parents. Both of them were raised in a lower-middle-class family. My dad started as a junior clerk in the Mumbai Police Department and worked hard to become an administrative officer before retiring. My mom became a supervisor in the women and child development sector of Maharashtra Shashan at 36 by appearing for a government exam and ranking in merit once she was free from children's responsibilities. She completed her master's in social work at 42, which is quite inspiring."

I saw my little sister pursuing her architectural studies in a tiny 180 sq ft room—smaller than a typical small room where four people could live. Think of a small room where four people could live. And let me tell you, it was smaller than that. Despite this, my parents were in higher positions in their government jobs. However, being a non-corrupt government servant in Mumbai, they struggled to afford a larger home. By God's grace, they saved diligently, took a loan, and bought a bigger house just a few years ago.

Yet, the size of the room was not our problem. My mental illness—paranoid schizophrenia and psychotic depression—caused significant challenges. I suffered from illusions and coped by abusing alcohol and drugs. This led to chaotic behaviour at home, where I would break things during episodes of mental turmoil. I am deeply grateful to my little sister for enduring these hardships caused by me, yet she never held any grudges and always supported me.

I am thankful for every part of this chaotic journey, especially to those who supported me unconditionally and even those who treated me negatively. I used every experience as a lesson, which has helped me gain wisdom, particularly about the Trimurti, the gods of Sanatana Dharma.

Ganapati Bappa blessed me with this theory and gave me a clear understanding of it on 28 September 2023 of Ganpati's Bappa's Visirjan. It was also the birth anniversary of the Islamic prophet Mohammed on the same day. Even though it was the end of the monsoon that day, it was raining heavily for a specific time, and there was deafening thunder in Mumbai. Some thoughts just got hit in my mind because of the chaotic nature present around me in the environment. It was as if everything had just been connected, and the discovery of this theory was clearly understood in my mind. It was like every dot that I had collected about life in my 10-year-long journey of chaotic mental illness just got connected to each other and gave me the ultimate theory of life. Suddenly, everything just stopped. The extreme rain and thunders were stopped. It was definitely a blessing. The years of observation, struggles, and suffering led to understanding this wisdom about life's ultimate truth, Hinduism, the Sanatana Dharma. Not in the form of a miracle, but after watching years of my mental struggle and will to solve it, I think Ganapati Bappa blessed me with this theory of the Trimurti way of life, which ultimately solved all my problems. I guarantee it will solve your problem logically without any miracles, but if you follow this theory, you will achieve miracles.

At last, I want to thank myself for always believing in me. For always being positive in the darkest chaotic moments of life, always learning something from every life's challenge and fatal fall. Always hoping that one day I am going to make it, and no matter how long it may take, I am ready to hustle. I embraced each depressed day's chaos as it's part of my journey to become something extraordinary in my life. I always used to find wisdom in how I could help mentally depressed people, even when I was facing chaotic depression problems.

I was steeped in the empathy of sorrows and walked on the road of fear. I fell several times into the pit of death, but I rose like a sweet morning, showing nothing had ever happened. I owned every aspect of my life as if I knew one day everything was going to be just a story, so I should rather embrace the correct wisdom from it.

I am no saint, sage, or monk in my real life. I am just a mere survivor of a chaotic mental illness, which created a difficult life for me. I consider myself a worrier, believer, greatest enjoyer, and giver in my life who fought with his mental illness to survive and live this incredible, beautiful life. I believe in science and not in overnight miracles but have total faith in the ultimate infallible spiritual energy, which I consider Lord Brahma the ultimate reality to which I connect through my inner pure soul, Lord Shiva, where I reach through control and detach mind which is Lord Vishnu.

Mr. Pranav Ashok Bharati Shinde is a government and United Nations-certified psychotherapist and hypnotherapist. He runs a YouTube channel dedicated to promoting fitness, psychology, and spirituality. In addition to his online efforts, he is actively involved in animal awareness and rescues snakes. He is very active in physical fitness and different types of meditation.

In his free time, Pranav provides counselling to drug addicts and individuals struggling with depression in his surroundings. Painting has been his favourite hobby since childhood. He is also passionate about motorbike riding and stunting. Moreover, he enjoys writing poems, shares, and quotes about life and spirituality, which he actively shares on his Instagram.

It is just the beginning for him; he is now exploring various things related to physical fitness, Mental awareness (Psychology), and Spiritual Awakening (Spirituality). He aims to build the best mental health App. Stay connected to him on social media for more updates.

Followed by youtube n insta:
YouTube: Pranava Mindful
Instagram: pranava_mindful

Milton Keynes UK
Ingram Content Group UK Ltd.
UKHW031204251124
451529UK00004B/231

9 798896 105435